My Problem
God's Opportunity

The story of my battle to overcome
Bone Marrow Cancer

By

Tim Johnson

PRESS

I dedicate this book to my wife Joan,
My most fervent desire is to love you the way you've loved me. You proved that for better or worse were not just words and that to rejoice in the Lord always is a choice which can be made no matter what.

And to my boys Kevin and Eric.
Thank you for your uncanny ability to find humor in everything and for teaching me that it wasn't just a wheel chair, it was a hand powered racer designed for hospital hallways.

Contents

Acknowledgement

I would like to express my appreciation to my niece, Stephanie Weckler, for all the work she has done in editing *My Problem, God's Opportunity*. Her editorial skills, incredible work ethic, and encouragement gave me the confidence to believe this book was possible. She handled my every mistake and rewrite with love and humor. No matter how many times I proved why I am a band director and not a writer, she found a way to make it work.

Forward

Tim Johnson asked if I would write a forward to his book, *My Problem, God's Opportunity*. It is truly a joy and an honor for me to have been asked by him.

I initially met Tim and Joan Johnson six years ago when he was referred to me by his medical oncologist to determine if reconstruction of his pelvis and his left hip was possible. Tim was suffering from an aggressive form of bone cancer, Multiple Myeloma. He underwent many treatments for his disease including systemic chemotherapy and two stem cell transplants. His disease, which affects bone marrow, had attacked many bones. It severely affected his pelvis and left hip, making sitting, standing, and walking extremely uncomfortable and nearly impossible.

Although Tim was visibly affected by his disease, he was both at peace and grateful for anything that we could offer as a treatment for his condition. He is a model patient and truly cares for us, his caregivers, as much as we care for him. Tim is a music teacher and band director. Like all excellent teachers, Tim is also a student and is continually learning new concepts so that he may better instruct his students. In this book, Tim relates what he learned from his severe illness, his difficult treatments, and his long recovery.

Tim not only teaches with his baton and pen, but he also teaches all of us through his life and attitude toward his circumstances and persons involved in his care. Tim truly exemplifies the "Fruits of the Spirit" described by St. Paul in his letter to the Galatians (Chapter 5, verses 22-24). These fruits are: love, joy, peace, patience, kindness, goodness, faithfulness, gentleness, and self-control. These characteristics in Tim's life come from his always-increasing faith in the Lord Jesus. All of his caregivers experienced these fruits of the Spirit of God in Tim's life as we treated him, and Tim truly cared about each of us.

As physicians and surgeons, we serve as conduits of God's healing powers. We may have recon-structed Tim's hip and pelvis, but God healed his bones, relieved his pain, and sent Tim's cancer into remission. I am both grateful and humbled to be used by God to help Tim and all of my patients.

Looking back at that initial meeting and consul-tation in 2003, I know now that they were not just "chance occurrences," but like everything in Tim's life and all of our lives, the meeting and consultation were directed by God to occur for His Purpose and His Glory.

Tim Johnson's book will be a blessing for your life. His story will show you that the problems in your life, both great and small, are opportunities for you to experience God's Power and God's Love in your life.

Donald A. Hackbarth, M.D., FACS
Department of Orthopaedic Surgery
Medical College of Wisconsin
February 24, 2009

And we know that all things work
together for good
to those who love God,
to those who are called according to
His purpose.
Romans 8:28

Giving thanks always for all things
to God the Father in the name of our
Lord Jesus Christ.
Ephesians 5:20

Rejoice always, pray without ceasing,
in everything give thanks;
for this is the will of God in Christ
Jesus for you.
I Thessalonians 5:16-18

How firm a foundation,
ye saints of the Lord,
Is laid for your faith
in His excellent Word!
What more can He say
than to you He hath said,
To you who for refuge to Jesus
have fled?

Fear not; I am with thee.
Oh, be not dismayed,
For I am thy God, I will still
give thee aid.
I'll strengthen thee help thee,
and cause thee to stand,
Upheld by my gracious,
omnipotent hand.

When thro' fiery trials
thy pathway shall lie,
My grace, all sufficient,
shall be thy supply.
The flames shall not hurt thee;
I only design
Thy dross to consume
and thy gold to refine.

The soul that on Jesus
hath leaned for repose
I will not, I will not desert to his foes;
That soul, tho' all hell should
endeavor to shake,
I'll never, no never, no never forsake.

From the hymn
How Firm a Foundation!

By George Keith

Chapter 1

I Have Cancer

You have cancer. These are words you don't really hear. When the doctor says "you have cancer," the words land on your skin and crawl all over you before they begin to sink in and crawl all over your insides. "You have cancer." The doctor could say *you*, but I had to say *I*. I couldn't put those words on someone else. I couldn't look at someone else and say *you*. I had to say *I*. *I have cancer.*

On February 20, 2002, my wife Joan and I were at St. Mary's hospital in Green Bay, Wisconsin. I had been sick for quite awhile and really wanted to get answers to our questions, but cancer was not what we were expecting. The doctor kept talking and I know I was listening, but I didn't remember anything—that is, until he said "it's multiple myeloma" (bone marrow cancer), and without treatments, I had just months to live. With treatments, I might live up to two years.

Multiple myeloma is a cancer that gets into the bone marrow. Bone marrow is a marshmallowy substance inside the bones that produces platelets along with red and white blood cells. Red blood cells carry the necessary oxygen to all the various organs in the body. White blood cells form the immune system. This explained why for the past year I'd been so tired and sick. My body's organs were dying from lack of oxygen, and my immune system was slowly withering away.

I was referred to Dr. Jaslowski of Green Bay Oncology at St. Mary's Hospital, and he went on to explain that the aches and pains in my body were due to the cancer causing my bone marrow to dry up. As the bone marrow dried up, so did the bones, and as the bones dried up, they were flaking away. This left my bones riddled with little holes, especially in my back, left hip and left femur (the bone connecting the knee to the hip).

There was more. I had a bulging disk in my spine that was pressing against my sciatic nerve. This was the reason for the constant, excruciating pain shooting through my back and down my left leg. My back was slowly compressing and becoming very brittle—so brittle that there was no possibility of any kind of operation. The risk to my spinal cord was too great.

We weren't finished yet. My hip and femur were literally disintegrating within my body. Flake by flake the bones were disappearing. All that I had left was a weak femur with a jagged tip and a deteriorating hip.

I called my parents and braced for the worst; instead, they provided the best. They were very calm and asked questions until they felt they understood the situation well enough to call other family members for Joan and me; and then they prayed. It was not a prayer of desperation but a simple prayer of love, authority, submission, and even praise. It was a prayer that still amazes me and often causes me to well up with tears at the thought of it. I know how much they love me, and yet despite the confusion and frustration they were feeling, all they expressed to God was trust. At the end of the prayer, my Dad said something that carried me through what would prove to be three years of constant battling to survive. "Tim, the question isn't whether God will be with you, but whether you will stay with God. Don't ever forget God already knows how this will turn out, and if you trust Him, it will be for good."

"If you trust Him it will be for good."[1] Over the next two-and-a-half years I clung to those words, I doubted those words, I begged God to help me believe, and I experienced God repeatedly prove them true.

When our two boys, Kevin (nine years old) and Eric (5 years old), came home from school that day, we sat them down on the couch and explained, as best we could, what was happening to me and what life would be like for us now. The hardest part with telling the boys was that we really had no idea what they were thinking or feeling. At their age, they couldn't put those kinds of thoughts and emotions into words. We prayed with them and let them know that we believed God would take care of all of us.

We were very concerned about them and kept in close contact with their teachers and the parents of the friends they played with to see if there was a change in behavior, or if the boys said anything to them. God blessed us with wonderful teachers and staff at Forest Glen Elementary School who kept a watchful eye over the boys and helped us get the boys through this with as many positive experiences as possible. Whenever we could, we took the boys with us to my doctor appointments, and we let them spend as much time as possible, with me at the hospital. We wanted them to meet the doctors and the nurses, and to see where I was at. As my ordeal with cancer grew, it seemed to help the boys that they knew who, and what we were talking about, and they loved the attention. The nurses were constantly sneaking ice cream and other treats to them, and on occasion even let them hold wheelchair races in the hallway. There are many things I'm grateful for as I look back on my time battling cancer, but at the top of the list is the number of positive memories the boys have of that time.

Informing My Students

The next day, I informed the people at the high school where I taught band that I had to stop work and begin treatments. Their immediate and over-whelming concern was for me and how to inform my students. As I stood before my students, I told them about the cancer. I explained in as much detail as I could what type of cancer I had, how it was affecting my body, and what the prognosis was.

I was holding up well until I asked the kids if they had any questions. At first, no one raised a hand. The room was completely silent. For the most part the students were still, most looking at me through teary eyes. I waited a couple moments longer, not sure what to do. It was obvious the kids were taking this really hard, and I began to pray, "God don't let this be a completely negative experience for the kids."

At that point one girl, Justine Hornick, raised her hand from the trumpet section. "Mr. Johnson, I have a question. Can I give you a hug?" This completely threw me. With tears in my eyes, I told her there was nothing I would like more. Student after student followed Justine to give me a hug or shake my hand. Most had a story to tell me about how something I had done had influenced their lives—little things that I had no recollection of. I had no idea how God had been using me to affect their lives, and without the cancer, I may never have known. In addition to the hugs and the stories, kids started to pray right there in the band room. Small groups of kids stood or sat together all around the band room praying together as they waited for their turn to talk with me. Student after student thanked me for my Christian faith and told me how much easier it was for them to believe knowing I did. I was completely overcome by the love the students poured out on me that morning. I really had no idea that the students had been watching me that closely.

As I left the school that day, I remember sitting in the car and crying. Not because of the cancer, but because of the love and energy I had just received from the students. I begged God to help me handle the cancer in a way that would be worthy of the respect they had just shown me. Later I heard story after story of how kids all over the school were going back to church just to pray for me. Parents were discussing faith and prayer with their sons and daughters around the dinner table or before going to bed at night. I was overwhelmed by the love my students and their parents expressed to me.

More Testing

Right after the band rehearsal, I headed back to the hospital for more tests. In one afternoon, I had a Muga Scan, MRI of the Spine, Full Skeletal Survey, and a Bone Marrow Biopsy. I remember the Bone

Marrow Biopsy best. Dr. Jaslowski and the attending nurse, Kim Klein, both informed me that this would hurt, possibly a lot. They described the procedure for me. First they would anesthetize the back of my left hip. Next, they would take a long needle, push it through my hip bone, and then suction out a sample of my bone marrow. After this, they would scrape my hip bone to remove a fragment for analysis.

I laid down on the table and Dr. Jaslowski went to work. Both Kim and Dr. Jaslowski are easy to talk with, so we talked while they worked. I really appreciated this as it took my mind off the procedure. I remember at one point, however, that Dr. Jaslowski stopped to inform me that he was about to start the most painful part. I braced myself, but was still totally unprepared for what I was about to feel. There are no words to describe the sharp pain that shot through my body. I remember thinking this would be a fantastic procedure to use if you wanted to torture someone. Then, just as suddenly, the pain ended.

Looking back on my experience, there are two main moments when I realized God had brought an incredible doctor and staff into my life. The first was when Dr. Jaslowski informed Joan and me that I had cancer. He took as much time with us as we needed, answering every question as clearly as he possibly could. I remember the compassion he had for Joan when he found out she had lost both her parents to cancer, in addition to possibly now losing her husband; and how he decided not to wait for the results of my tests to come back from the lab (telling us whether or not I had cancer), but walked to the lab himself to get the results as soon as they were available.

The second moment was as I lay there on the table during that first Bone Marrow Biopsy. With Dr. Jaslowski and Kim, I was obviously in great hands medically, but I was also coming to realize what wonderful, caring people they were. They got the bone and bone marrow samples on the first try, and did everything they possibly could to help me through the procedure. I didn't know it then, but I was to have seven Bone Marrow Biopsies in the next two and a half years. I grew to really appreciate the skilled, compassionate hands that perform necessary, but painful procedures.

On Friday, February 22, in preparation for chemo, a central line or catheter was surgically placed in my chest. A central line is a tube with one end inserted into an artery and the other end sticking out of the person's chest. A simple yet effective valve is placed at the end of the catheter to keep blood from pouring out of the artery. The catheter can be used to draw blood or to act as an IV that inserts medicine, such as chemo, into the body.

Informing Our Church

On Sunday morning, church had a different feel to it. We had called our church immediately after talking with my parents to let them know that we would no longer be able to teach our four-year-old year old Sunday school class. We were placed on the church prayer chain, and Pastor Arni Jacobson, the senior pastor at Bayside Church in Green Bay, let us know that he would like to have us come up front for prayer during the service. Midway through the first service, Pastor Arni informed the church of my diagnosis. After anointing Joan and I with oil, [2] the leaders of the church came up to pray for us. A visiting minister, who just happened to be speaking that day on God's ability to bring healing, led the congregation in prayer.

It was hard on me to sit in the sanctuary during the first service and know that we were done teaching Sunday School. I mentioned this to Lori Englebert, our church's pre-school director between services. She informed me that the teacher for one of the class-rooms wasn't able to make it that morning, and she asked if I felt up to doing it. She didn't need to ask twice. It was amazing how much energy I suddenly felt at the thought of getting to teach one last time. I remember sitting as much as I could and being very thankful for the teenage helpers in the room, but I made it. I got to teach one last time. It felt like a gift from God, and I had no idea how God was bringing this to the attention of the entire congregation during the second service. While I went to work in the pre-school area, Joan decided to also attend the second service. So many people from the first service were asking questions that Joan couldn't get back into the sanctuary until well after the service had started.

Pastor Arni informed those attending the second service about the cancer, and asked for me, but I wasn't there. Joan and I didn't know that he was hoping to pray for us during both services. He made a comment to the congregation about seeing me just before the service and said something to the effect of, "come on Tim, I know you're here somewhere." At that point, Joan spoke up and informed Pastor Arni and the congregation that I had a chance to teach Sunday School one last time and took it. From what I've been told, this really touched the heart of the congregation. I didn't intend for that to happen. I didn't intend for anyone to even know that I was teaching, but God arranged for it to be known. This was one of my first glimpses into how God can take something even like cancer and arrange it for his purposes.

Chapter 2

First Treatments

Starting Chemotherapy

Thursday morning, February 28, Joan and I drove to St. Mary's Hospital for my first chemo treatment. We walked into the oncology treatment room and found an open area to sit in. There were half-a-dozen recliners for the patients to use and regular chairs for the non-patients. Each recliner had a small, 9 inch TV hanging just to the side of the chair on an adjustable arm. I looked around the room. Most of the patients were considerably older than me and had a variety of looks on their faces. Some looked very relaxed as they watched TV, read books, or talked with the people around them. Others had an anxious aura about them, questioning or complaining about everything. I remember wondering what they were thinking about me. Could they tell this was my first time getting chemo? Did I look nervous? Did I look anxious? I had no idea what to expect. I tried not to stare, but I found myself watching everyone as I tried to figure out what I was about to go through.

The nurse came up to us, introduced herself, showed us the equipment I was going to use, and began to explain the procedure. I was given a portable chemo pack to take home. The chemo and pump were in a fanny pack that also had a shoulder harness. A small, one-fourth inch hose coming out of the pump was attached to the catheter in my chest and pumped the chemo into my blood stream over the course of four days. Since the hose was attached to both the catheter and the chemo pump, I had to carry the chemo pack wherever I went. I usually used the shoulder harness.

Carrying the chemo pack around was a bit of a nuisance and kind of awkward, but I was very grateful to be able to use it. By using the chemo pack, I was able to get the chemo I needed over the course of four days. Without the chemo pack, I would have been required to get all my medicine in one day, while sitting for hours in the oncology treatment room, and getting the chemo in a much higher dose. The amount of chemo I was getting was the same either way, but the hope was that by getting the chemo in smaller doses, I wouldn't get as sick.

However, I did get sick with chemo-related nausea, vomiting, and light- headedness, especially nausea. No matter what I did, I was nauseous. Even while laying down and taking deep breaths, I was nauseous. Sitting up was very hard, and the only walking I did was to go to the bathroom to throw up. I kept a small plastic garbage can right next to the bed and wound up using it quite often.

First Hospital Stay

Saturday night I began to notice there was a growing numbness in my left leg from the thigh down. It was getting harder and harder to move my leg, and the pain in my back was intensifying. By Sunday afternoon I could hardly move, and I was beginning to feel feverish. I wanted to lie down, so I climbed the stairs to our bedroom, half using and half dragging my left leg. Making it to the bed, I fell asleep.

When I woke up a couple hours later, my leg wouldn't move. Joan, Kevin, and Eric came running upstairs to help me, but I was in too much pain to move, and my leg couldn't hold any weight. I needed to get to the hospital, but we needed more help. There was no way I was getting downstairs on my own, so Joan called for an ambulance.

The men from the ambulance crew got me downstairs and out to the ambulance before taking me to St. Vincent Hospital. The next morning,

Dr. Jaslowski brought in a back specialist who explained in detail just how bad my back was. He described the type of surgery that would be required to fix my back and how impossible it was due to the brittleness of my spine. There was just too much risk to the spinal cord. They would try to control my pain as best they could with medication, but there was really nothing else that they could do.

Before going home, Dr. Jaslowski ordered a walker for me. The numbness had subsided some, but the pain in my leg and back were always there in varying degrees. Sometimes I could walk with a cane, but usually I needed the walker to move around. At this point there was absolutely no way I was going to get to our bed upstairs, so Dr. Jaslowski ordered a hospital bed to be placed in our living room and allowed me to go home.

Nausea and Fever

I was very excited about getting home that day since it was Joan's birthday and the last place I wanted to be was in the hospital. Unfortunately, my time at home proved to be very short. Things went fairly well for a couple of days, but by Sunday, March 10, my 42 birthday, we knew I needed to see a doctor. My temperature was climbing, I was throwing up, and I was too dizzy to move, so Joan took me to the St. Mary's emergency room where they had me admitted to the hospital.

Once in the hospital, I started to feel better. I stopped vomiting and began to get my energy back; so much so that I even made it down the hallway to take a shower Wednesday and Thursday. But no matter what the doctors and nurses tried, my temperature would not return to normal.

All week long I told the doctors that I really wanted to make it home by Friday, March 15, since that was Eric's sixth birthday. Joan and the boys were already going through enough because of the cancer, and I didn't want to make Eric celebrate his birthday in a hospital room. Dr. Saphner, a colleague of Dr. Jaslowski's at Green Bay Oncology, was on duty that day and arranged for me to go home. My temperature still wasn't normal, but it was down and I was feeling stronger. Joan and I left with strict instructions from Dr. Saphner to take my temperature every couple of hours and to call them immediately if it started going up again.

The following Wednesday I did have a higher temperature again, so we called Dr. Jaslowski. Using ice and Tylenol, we were able to bring the temperature down a little, but that all changed on Thursday when my temperature soared to 105 degrees. I was once again admitted into St. Mary's Hospital.

I don't really remember much about what happened next. I remember being in a hospital room with all the windows open, and I remember some ice on my legs. Other than that, I was delusional. I found out later that my memories of that night are of things that never happened.

My temperature was hanging around 106 degrees, and there didn't seem to be anything that could be done to bring it down. Multiple nurses, plus Joan, were giving me constant attention. I was dying. The windows were indeed open and I was packed in ice. Despite this, I still complained of being hot. Due to the weakness of my internal organs and having almost no immune system, I wasn't expected to live through the night. I'm alive today because of the love poured over me by Joan and the nurses.

The next day it was determined that the catheter, which had become infected, would have to be removed. The infection from the catheter was the reason for my high temperature and was literally killing me. Once the catheter was removed, the infection quickly healed and my temperature returned to normal. By Friday, March 26, I was strong enough to have a new catheter inserted. This time they put a PICC line in my left arm, just below the shoulder. This proved to be more uncomfortable, but it had a much lower chance of infection than the chest catheter.

I was still extremely weak and could no longer walk with the cane. The walker was there for me to use, but I rarely had the energy to walk far even with that, so Dr. Jaslowski ordered a wheelchair for me. That day I was determined to walk with the walker, so I got out of bed and headed down the hospital hallway. I would walk a few feet and rest; walk a few feet and rest, over and over until I got to the end of the hallway. Complicating my walk was that I had to bring the IV machine with me. By the end of the hallway I was totally exhausted.

I sat down in some chairs by the elevator and tried to get my energy back. People came and went getting on and off the elevator, and I actually enjoyed saying "hi" to people, or at least nodding to them as they walked by, but I was beginning to realize that sitting was also making me tired. My body just seemed drained of all strength.

Fighting discouragement, I got up and started the 25 yard walk back to my room. I wanted my bed. I needed my bed, but first I had to get to the room. I would walk a few feet, stop, and rest; walk a few feet, stop, and rest. Nurses would ask me how I was doing and I would try to look as energetic as possible and say "fine". (I learned after this to be more honest with the nurses in the future.) About halfway back to my room, one of the nurses held me up under my left arm and pushed the IV machine for me. With her help I made it back to the room and collapsed onto the bed. God bless nurses everywhere!

<u>Carolyn</u>

The next day, with the PICC line in place and my temperature normal, I was discharged to go home. My sister-in-law Carolyn, a nurse from Kankakee,

IL, came and spent a week with us. A couple of years later she revealed that when she came, she was fully expecting those to be my final hours and wanted to be there for Joan when it happened. Having her at home was a real boost for all of us. She took time to explain in detail how the different drugs worked, and why I needed them in the doses prescribed; and she walked with me—not long walks though. Our walks were from the living room, where my bed was, around the kitchen table, and back to the bed. We celebrated the time I made it twice around the kitchen table.

For the most part, the only time I would get out of bed was to go to the bathroom. The bathroom was only about twenty feet from the bed, but it took all my energy to get there. Carolyn had me rest at the kitchen table, which was about half way to the bathroom, and then continue when I was ready.

Before heading back, I would often put the toilet seat down and just sit there trying to get enough energy to make it the twenty feet back to bed. When I felt strong enough, I'd grab the walker, get up, walk to the kitchen table, sit and rest, walk to the bed, and collapse in exhaustion. My spirits remained high while Carolyn was with us, but after she left, no matter how hard I battled, I felt myself falling further into discouragement. As the days dragged on, I found myself looking back on how I got to this point, and longing for life to be the way it used to be.

Chapter 3

Looking Back

I remember a warm August evening in 2000. We had just moved into our new house at the end of February, and I was working in the back yard. Joan and I decided we should move the jungle gym from where we had it on the west side of the yard to the east side. Our boys, Kevin then 7, and Eric who was 4, liked the idea of the move since it would put the jungle gym in the shade and open up more of the yard to run around in. As I completed the move, I felt a pain in my hip and thought I'd pulled a muscle from all the lifting and moving I had done that day. Unconcerned, I went in the house to relax.

As I look back on that day now, I often wonder how different my life would be if at that moment, I had known I wasn't feeling a pulled muscle. If only I'd known it was the first sign of a very dangerous cancer. What if we had caught it in the initial stages before it could ravage my body? How many things would I still be able to do that I now can't? How much pain would I have been able to avoid? How much easier would life have been for Joan, the boys, and me if only we'd known right then that it was cancer? But we didn't know. As far as I was concerned I had a pulled muscle. I got up the next morning and went on with my life.

It was a life I thoroughly enjoyed. Kevin was entering second grade at the school district in which I was a band director. Eric was getting set to join a new pre-school, and Joan was busy converting our new front room into a piano studio for her 30 + students. Our property butted up against an old railroad track bed that had been converted into a hiking and biking trail. In the evenings, we would love to go for short walks on the trail or have a bonfire in our back yard.

One Sunday at church, our pastor Arni Jacobson informed the congregation that the church was in need of adult teachers in the pre-school area. At the end of the service Joan and I walked out of the sanctuary and talked about praying to see if this was something God wanted us do. The closer we got to the pre-school area to pick up Eric, the more uncomfortable I became with praying about this. We didn't need to pray about it, we needed to do it! Here we were, two teachers, wondering if God wanted us to fulfill the need four-year-olds had to learn about Jesus. What did we think God was going to tell us? "No! My will is to have you sit in the sanctuary while the overworked people that are currently teaching, continue to be grossly over-worked." I strongly believe in waiting on the Lord for the leading of the Holy Spirit. This one, however, didn't take a mighty move of God to figure out. We needed to do this.

Joan and I couldn't believe how scared we were as we entered our Sunday School classroom for the first time. These were four-year-old kids. I had been teaching middle school and high school kids for 17 years, and I loved it. Why was I so afraid of these kids? Joan had been teaching piano for a number of years and was used to working with kids from eight years old on up. Yet she was feeling the same fear I was. These four-year-olds scared us!

We spent more time praying over those kids than I think I've ever prayed in my life. I would love to say we were praying deep spiritual prayers asking God to please bring spiritual insight to these four-year-olds, but I have to admit it was mainly, "God, help us survive. Please don't let them hurt us or destroy the room." As always, God answered our prayer and then some.

We grew to love our time with those kids. Eric was actually one of our students and Kevin loved to come in with us and help. I'll never forget the time Joan drew a life-size picture of Goliath and had the kids stand up against it to be measured. Or the time we brought 12 different Teddy bears to play the part of Joseph's[4] family and Eric introduced his Winnie the Pooh Bear as a special visiting TV star to play the part of Joseph.

Kevin had a wonderful Teddy Bear named Booboo (because he reminded us of Yogi's Booboo.) Each week, just before story time, Kevin would sneak behind a three foot high curtain. With one hand he'd hold Booboo up for the kids to see, and with the other hand he held a microphone that he would speak into. The night before, Kevin and I would work up a routine with Kevin (who was hidden from view) speaking as Booboo. Each week we would have Booboo ask a question a four-year-old might ask, and then I would answer Booboo with a bible story. Kevin got so good at talking and moving Booboo that the kids actually believed Booboo could talk. On one occasion, one of the kids asked me a question I couldn't answer and later went to Booboo to see if he knew.

As the months went by, I was having more and more trouble with hip and back pain. On at least six occasions I went to the doctor and was assured that it was nothing that exercise, heat, and relaxation couldn't fix. I faithfully did everything I was told and believed that God would take care of the pain, but it kept getting worse.

Some days I would get up, hardly able to move, and I found myself getting tired in the middle of the day—and not just a little tired. There were days when I couldn't go on without a nap. By the time lunch would come I would be so tired that I needed to skip lunch and take a nap. Joan and I couldn't understand what was going on, but we were trusting that God would take care of me and that my energy would come back and the pains would go away.

But the pains didn't go away. They got worse and every day it seemed harder for me to find the energy to make it through work. We saw the doctor again and this time she ran the series of tests that found the cancer. I didn't know how to react. I felt calm, but this wasn't fair. Why me? With every ounce of everything within me, I wanted my old life back.

Chapter 4

God's Hand on My Life

<u>Battling Depression</u>

Depression is real! Until the cancer, I had a cavalier attitude about depression: If you're thinking about something that depresses you, then just stop thinking about it—but that didn't work. I tried to control my thoughts, but I couldn't. The words just kept shrilling in my head, *you're worthless, you're worthless, you're worthless, you're worthless.*

A couple of weeks after Carolyn left, I was so weak from the cancer and the chemo treatments that I could hardly make it out of bed to go to the bathroom. I felt totally worthless. I was a nuisance and a burden to everyone in my life, especially my wife and two young sons.

At night, when the house was entirely quiet, my thoughts would become unbearable. All I could think about was how much pain I was bringing into the lives of the people I loved the most, and how much extra work I was causing for my wife. She loved me so much and just kept working and giving, while all I could do was take. I could accomplish nothing for her or anyone else. I was worthless. [5]

Those thoughts would pierce straight through me. *I'm worthless. Worthless as a husband, worthless as a father, worthless as a friend. I've tried to serve God all my life and this is what I get in return. I'm now a burden to everyone. Why serve God? If this is what I get, why serve God?*

Those thoughts left my head spinning, whirling faster and faster. The thoughts seemed alive. I couldn't argue with them. They seemed true. I was worthless. *Why serve God? Why live?* I tried to pray, but all I could come up with was, *why bother? God doesn't care about me. God might love other people, but He's abandoned me. He might answer other people's prayers, but He obviously won't answer mine.* Faster and faster and with a growing intensity the thoughts would beat me down each night.

I was growing weaker, in body and faith, until one night the thoughts scared me. *Why not just die?* I tried to pray, but I couldn't formulate a prayer through the thoughts. *God doesn't care. I'm worthless. Just die.* It seemed as if the thoughts weren't my own. As if they had a different source all their own. These didn't seem like thoughts any longer—they felt like commands.

Jesus. I tried to start a prayer, but that was as far as I could get my mind to go. *Jesus.* I tried again. Over and over again I tried to pray. *Jesus, Jesus, Jesus,* but that was as far as my mind would go. *I'm worthless, just die.* I kept saying *Jesus, Jesus, Jesus, Jesus.* I was no longer praying, I was clinging to that word, that name, Jesus. Jesus was the only positive thought in my mind. *I'm worthless. Jesus. Just die. Jesus.*

I have no idea how long the battle went on, but it wasn't a short time. Looking back on that time, I now realize it was the power of the name of Jesus versus the power of darkness. At that moment, however, it was just my desire to live versus the desire to die, and the name of Jesus is all that kept me alive. Praise God, I'll never know for sure, but I often wonder if I would have died that night if not for the name of Jesus. There was no big prayer—in fact, no little prayer—just His name.

That night, I learned there is power in the name of Jesus. I'm not sure how or when it happened, but all of a sudden I was waking up. It was morning and I'd slept through the remainder of the night. No more nightmares, no more negative thoughts about dying. I felt great, and for the first time I knew God was with me and I could trust Him. It was no longer something I believed, it was something I knew!

I still felt worthless, however. I needed something to do. Something that I could do that would help Joan, even a little. But what? It seems comical now, but it was a major revelation for me the moment I realized I could clean the bathrooms' sinks and toilets.

Joan got out the cleaning supplies for me, and I made my way into the bathroom, taking a pillow with me. Sitting on a stool, I cleaned the sink and then knelt down next to the toilet. By this time I needed to rest, so I would put the pillow on the toilet seat and rest my head on the pillow. When I felt strong enough, I would start to clean the toilet. Usually I would have to rest one more time before I got the toilet clean, but I did it. I could do something. I could clean the sinks and toilets. It might not seem like anything to most people, but right then to me it meant I wasn't worthless. I could help Joan.

I called my Mom to tell her I was cleaning, and I could feel her excitement for me. She started to laugh when she heard what an involved process this "simple" job was for me and called for my dad to come to the phone. He, too, was excited for me as I told him I no longer felt worthless. He then told me something I'll never forget. "Tim, you're definitely not worthless. You can do what might be the most valuable thing of all. You can show people how to serve the Lord in the middle of tough times. You can show your kids at school how to handle a problem like this."

From that moment on, I became determined to make it back to school as often as I could to talk to the students and let them know how I was doing. The other teachers were great about letting me come in and talk to the kids whenever I had the energy to do so, and because of the incredible miracles God was doing in my life, it was just natural to talk about God.

God's Healing

Little by little I started to gain some strength back and began to think about going to church. It took awhile, but finally one Friday evening in late April I made it. While my leg and back were extremely sore and each step produced sharp pains, my desire to get out of the house and make it to church was definitely stronger. So with the help of my cane, I slowly limped into church.

Toward the end of the service, Pastor Arni called me up to the front of the church and had me sit in the front pew. As people gathered around me, Pastor Arni led them in prayer. At first I was just energized by being with people again. The warmth of having that many people concerned about me and praying for me overwhelmed me.

As Pastor Arni placed his hand on my head, however, the energy changed. I felt what I can only describe as shooting warmth or an electrical charge shoot down my back and through my left leg. Immediately, I knew that something had just happened. My leg, which had been shrinking due to the disappearance of the bone, felt longer, and my back had a tingling sensation that continued for a long period of time.

I didn't know what to think. I was very thankful for the prayers everyone was praying for me, and I knew God could answer, but never in my wildest dreams did I really believe He would. I was stunned. At the end of the prayer I got up and realized I was shaking. My mind was spinning in circles trying to grasp what was happening to me. As I walked to the back of the church I realized that my left leg, while still shorter then my right leg, was definitely longer than when I had walked to the front of the church just minutes before.

I was afraid to say anything to anybody because I wasn't sure people would believe me. We might have prayed that this miracle would happen, but I wasn't sure anyone actually thought it would. The longer I walked, however, the more obvious it became to me that my body was changing. My left leg had compressed to the point that when I walked, I would lean and sway heavily in that direction. Now as I walked, my limp, while definitely still there, wasn't nearly as noticeable. With a mixture of excitement, astonishment, awe, and confusion, I started to let people know what was happening to me.

Over the course of the next three days, the pain in my back entirely disappeared and the shooting pain in my leg softened. I gained a considerable amount of my strength back, and for the next 16 months I was able to walk with just the aid of a cane. It wasn't until a few months later, however, that I fully grasped what had happened to me.

On January 28, 2003, Joan and I met with Dr. Hackbarth of Froedtert Hospital in Milwaukee to discuss the possibility of having my hip and femur replaced. Beyond fortunate, we felt blessed to be working with someone like Dr. Hackbarth - a musculoskeletal oncologist (orthopaedic oncologist) who serves as the Director of Musculoskeletal Oncology in the Department of Orthopaedic Surgery at the Medical College of Wisconsin and Froedtert Hospital. With his credentials and twenty years of experience dealing with patients with multiple myeloma and their reconstructive problems, we knew we were in good hands.

In preparation for this appointment, I had my first full skeletal exam in months. During the appointment, Dr. Hackbarth hung the x-rays and asked me how I was sitting. At the time, I was sitting on the examining table and wasn't sure I understood the question, so Dr. Hackbarth asked me again. "How are you sitting?" I muttered something about my legs, back, and arms, but I still didn't understand the question, so I didn't know what to say.

Next, Dr. Hackbarth asked me how I had come into the examining room. Still not understanding his line of questioning, I replied that I had walked in from the parking lot with the use of the cane. Dr. Hackbarth looked me straight in the eyes and, asked, "You walked in from the parking lot?" What could I say but yes? Next he asked how much pain I was in. I told him that the pain was considerable, but tolerable.

Then he showed us the x-rays. First we looked at my right leg, which was an example of what a leg should look like. Then he showed us the left leg. Immediately we understood his questions. Three-fourths of my hip was gone, and the whole top of the femur had also disappeared. What remained of the tip of the femur was just a sharp, jagged bone that was flopping around inside of what was left of my hip. I should have been in excruciating pain. I should have been bed-ridden, and there was absolutely no way I should have been able to walk anywhere with just the help of a cane, much less walk in from the parking lot.

He then asked us how we had discovered the cancer. We explained about my back problems including the bulging disk in my spine. With that he said "Oh yes, I think I can see where the bulging disk was." Joan and I looked at each other and said "*was?*" For the first time we really realized that the bulging disk was no longer causing me pain, and hadn't been for quite awhile. In addition, most of the holes and pit marks in my spine had disappeared. We were looking at what was close to a normal back!

Just a few months earlier I was told that nothing could be done for me. My back was inoperable. Yet now, without any medical intervention whatsoever, I was looking at a mostly normal back. The impossible had happened. I had a new back! Furthermore, I was walking miraculously on a leg with basically no hip and one-third of the femur missing.

The news continued as Dr. Hackbarth informed us that he liked the way my broken pelvic bone had healed. Now it was my turn for questions. "What broken pelvic bone?" Again he showed us the x-ray and pointed to a straight line across the left side of my pelvic bone. It was obvious that at some point I'd had a broken pelvic bone and that it had healed perfectly. There was only one problem. I never knew I had a broken pelvic bone!

I'm told that a broken pelvic bone is very painful. Sometime during the months that passed between skeletal exams, my pelvic bone had completely broken in two and healed up again without me even knowing anything was wrong. Not only was my femur jagged, sharp, and flopping around inside a hip that was three-fourths gone, the pelvic bone was also broken. I was walking around on it with only the use of a cane and was completely oblivious that anything was wrong. God had healed my back and my broken pelvic bone with absolutely no medical intervention!

It took awhile to come down from the spiritual high I was on, but I eventually did. I didn't know it at the time, but in addition to showing me what He was capable of doing, God was also showing me that a close relationship with Him is much more rewarding than a fantastic, miraculous healing, and that a fantastic, miraculous healing does not automatically build a closer relationship with God. My back was healed, but my leg wasn't. God had just taken a good share of the pain away. Later, other problems surfaced that left me completely and utterly confused.

Chapter 5

First Stem Cell Transplant

I'm In Remission!!

Through May and June, I continued with my chemo treatments, and then at the beginning of July, I went through a series of tests to find out exactly where I was at with the multiple myeloma. On July 9, 2002, Joan and I walked into the clinic not knowing what to expect. I had blood drawn at the beginning of each visit to the oncology clinic, and over the last couple of months, the lab results were showing definite improvement. I also knew I was feeling better, so we were really hoping the tests results would come back showing a drastic reduction of the cancer. Dr. Jaslowski walked into the clinic patient room where we had been waiting and informed us that he had good news. Not only was I showing improvement, I was officially in remission!

It's hard to explain the exhilaration one feels when hearing the words *you're in remission*. In February, I was told that I had just months to live and now, six months later, I was in remission. I think I could feel every organ in my body breathe a sigh of relief. My face—completely on its own, without any thought or urging from me—broke into a huge grin. I looked Dr. Jaslowski straight in the eye and my vocal chords started vibrating in just the right way to produce very short words: "Wow!!" "Really?" "Are you sure?" "Wow!!"

I would imagine I said more than this, but I'm also pretty sure I wasn't any more articulate than that. It didn't really matter what I was saying however—I WAS IN REMISSION! Thank goodness Joan was there because Dr. Jaslowski had more very important information to share with us.

Even though I was in remission, my battling was a long way from over. This was just the first battle of the war. It was a huge victory, but now I needed to prepare for the next battle. The cancer had almost totally destroyed my immune system, leaving me very susceptible to a relapse. Dr. Jaslowski recommended a procedure in which I would receive two stem cell transplants. The first one would require the harvesting and transplanting of my own stem cells, and the second would require a stem cell transplant from a sibling. In both cases, the goal was to have the stem cells produce new bone marrow, which would produce the needed platelets, red blood cells, and white blood cells to give me a new immune system.

Since there wasn't a facility in Green Bay that performed the stem cell transplants I needed, Dr. Jaslowski recommended two hospitals for us to choose from. One was UW Hospital in Madison, WI, and the other was Froedtert Memorial Lutheran Hospital in Milwaukee, WI. My brother Wally lived in Milwaukee, so Joan and I decided on Froedtert Hospital.

Dr. Vesole

Arrangements were made for us to see the Bone Marrow Transplant unit where I would live during treatments, and to meet our new doctor, Dr. Vesole, on July 19. Joan and I were to meet with Dr. Vesole around one o'clock in the afternoon. At two o'clock, we were still waiting when a nurse came in and informed us that Dr. Vesole was running behind but should be able to get to us soon. Around two-thirty, another nurse came in to let us know that Dr. Vesole had been called to another part of the hospital due to an emergency. Finally around four o'clock we got to meet Dr. Vesole, and it was worth every minute of the wait.

Here was a man, considered to be among the most brilliant in the world in the area of multiple myeloma, taking all the time Joan and I needed to have all our questions answered. He was concerned about every aspect of our lives. Was I doing okay psychologically and emotionally? How was Joan holding up? How were the boys doing? Did we have good insurance? Were we getting support from family and friends? Besides my medical needs, was there anything else he could do for us? Even though we had just met him, he talked to us as if we were family or close friends.

He explained to us the options we had. Basically, there were two: wait for the cancer to reoccur and fight it off with treatments again and again until I died, or enter a clinical trial group. The particular trial group he had in mind was experimenting with a new procedure to fight the reoccurrence of multiple myeloma. This was a continuation of work performed by a clinical trial group in Seattle, Washington.

Harvesting Stem Cells

On August 16, I was to have my stem cells harvested. To make sure these stem cells were cancer free; I received another massive round of chemo on August 1. This led to nausea, fever, and the loss of every hair on my body, but I made it through fairly well, and on the morning of August 16, I headed back to Milwaukee to have my stem cells harvested. Feeling nervous, but strong and ready to go, I walked in.

I laid down on a hospital bed and the nurses began preparing me for the procedure. A machine with two hoses attached, one on each side, was wheeled up to the foot of the bed. A needle attached to one of the hoses was inserted into a vein in my left arm. The other hose was attached to a vein in my right arm. The blood was drawn from my left arm and flowed into the machine which separated my stem cells from the blood. Once this step was completed, the blood flowed back into my body through my right arm. I felt like a car getting an oil change. It didn't hurt, but it did take several hours. To pass the time away, they had a number of recent movies I could choose from to watch.

From the time my stem cells were collected, I had to wait one month before I could have them reintroduced back into my body. I spent that month preparing myself as best I could for my hospital stay. I knew I would be in a private room on a sterile floor. Because of my weak immune system, it was very important that I not be exposed to germs. My body needed all the strength it could muster just to get the reintroduced stem cells to form new bone marrow, and to get the new bone marrow to start producing blood cells and platelets at a higher level. I knew I would have a TV, VCR, and telephone in my room, but other than this I really didn't know what to expect. In dealing with the cancer, I discovered time and again a simple truth: the unknown can be a major source of fear and apprehension, and this was proving to be no exception. I tried to plan for what was coming, but it was hard.

I packed favorite books or things I had wanted to read but never had the time to do so. (I would have plenty of time now.) I recorded episodes of Hogan's Heroes, Beverly Hillbillies, Dick VanDyke, Home Improvement, and other shows to watch. I bought John Wayne movies and picked out other favorite movies we owned. I had a CD player, cassette player, radio, and picked out favorite music and messages to keep with me. No matter how hard I tried to prepare myself though, there was one fact I couldn't escape. I really had no idea what to expect.

<u>Stem Cell Transplant Patient</u>

Monday, September 16, I walked into Froedtert Memorial Lutheran Hospital with no idea when I would get to leave again. We'd been told to expect that I would be in the hospital for a minimum of four weeks, but that I could be there for quite a bit longer. My time alone was to begin soon since Joan and the boys would have to head back to Green Bay right after I was settled in my room.

I was free to move about on the floor, but due to the pain in my left hip and thigh bone, I didn't feel like leaving my room very much. Once in awhile I would walk to the end of the hall and back, but that was about it. Most of my days and nights were spent watching TV, listening to music, and sleeping. But

I want to be careful not to give the impression that I was resting. One does not catch up on sleep or rest in a hospital.

I learned during previous hospital stays that it is impossible to sleep or rest for more than two hours at a time in a hospital, and Froedtert was proving to be no different. Every couple of hours a nurse would come in to take my temperature, listen to my heart, and take my pulse. Other visits from hospital staff were to clean the room, perform repairs, change the bed sheets, draw blood, bring meals, or my favorite, to wake me up and ask how much pain I was feeling on a scale of one to ten. Of course, I hadn't been feeling any pain—I was sleeping. But now that I was awake I could feel the pain again.

At first I looked at these interruptions as a nuisance and I would catch myself getting annoyed, especially when I had just fallen asleep and they would wake me up. But it didn't take long for my opinion to change. These nurses and the majority of the hospital staff were always on the go; always serving and always doing their work with a high level of excellence.

I'd hear a patient somewhere down the hall chew out a nurse for some relatively meaningless thing and then have her walk into my room, still serving, still working with a high level of excellence, and still pleasant. I began to notice how many patients each nurse was responsible for and grew amazed at their ability to complete each job and then move on to the next. To clean out a bed pan here, deliver a meal there, help someone get out of bed and support them as they walked to the bathroom, pass out the right medications in the right doses to everyone, fill out an endless array of forms, bring water or a popsicle, counsel patients struggling with their emotions and/ or thoughts, answer endless questions, etc. They did all this while trying to live their own lives with their own problems. My admiration for the hospital staff grew every day. (Except the people who came around at two-thirty in the morning with those big zamboni-like floor cleaning vehicles. Is that really necessary at that time of the night??)

In the middle of the second day, two nurses walked into my room to give me my stem cell infusion. They hooked an IV into the catheter that had been inserted into my chest and hung what looked like a big bag of blood onto an IV pole. I was expecting more than this. For some reason I thought I would be wheeled into a big laboratory with lots of monitors and big machines humming all around the room. At the very least, I thought they would need to wheel a few of those things into my room.

I was a little disappointed, but relieved at the same time. I'd been hooked up to scores of IVs. This was nothing new. IVs had never bothered me before. I remember thinking *I can get through this, no problem it's just an IV*, and for a little bit that was true. It didn't take long, however, for the side effects to kick in. I was nauseous, had no energy, and almost everything tasted the same—bland.

Each morning I was supposed to take a shower, but it was hard. I had no energy. Because of my hip, it took everything I had just to get out of bed, and standing really made me dizzy. In addition, mornings were also when I felt the most nauseous. I know it's not a pretty picture, but most mornings I'd wait until I needed to throw up and/or use the bathroom and then as long as I was in the bathroom, I'd take my shower.

Fortunately, the shower had a bench I could sit on, so I would sit on the bench to undress and then start the water. Often I would sit and let the water pour on me without moving a muscle. I was just too tired, nauseous, and dizzy to move, and the water felt so good. When I felt a spurt of energy I would wash my hair or try to really clean up. The worst part was when I needed to throw up while showering. For this reason, I learned to keep a small garbage can right next to the shower.

Around lunch time, I would usually start to feel a little more energetic and I'd get dressed. The hospital staff would encourage me to get out of the hospital gown and into my own clothes whenever possible. It amazed me how much getting dressed in regular clothes helped me feel a sense of normalcy. It was just jeans and a t-shirt or sweatshirt, but it really gave me a boost of energy. There was something about being able to get out of hospital garb that gave me a feeling of making progress. There were a couple of days when I just didn't have the energy to get dressed, but I tried hard not to let that happen.

Passing Time

It didn't take me long to realize that controlling my thoughts would be the most important (and most difficult) part of getting better. It's amazing the things your thoughts can wander to when you have as much time by yourself as I did. I would try to read, but during the first few days after the stem cell transplant, I was too nauseous and dizzy to read for more than just a few minutes at a time. I watched a lot of TV, but even watching the things I brought with me got pretty old after awhile. So often I would just lie in bed and think.

I would think about my family, my job, places I would rather be, and things that I couldn't have or do in the hospital. Letting my mind dwell on things like that made it easy to get down, or even depressed, and I couldn't afford to get depressed. I already knew how depression could negatively affect my ability to get better, and I wanted to get better. I wanted to go home. Depression was as big an enemy to me as battling the effects of cancer. The problem with the depression was that it was mainly in my head. How does one control their thoughts in this type of situation?

I decided my first goal would be to always be cheerful with the nurses; maybe not always happy, but at least cheerful. This didn't mean I would lie to the nurses about how I was doing—I needed to let them know exactly what was happening with me—but I wasn't going to dwell on the negative either. I would lie in bed and no matter how I was feeling, I would force myself to find something that was better than the day before. When the nurses came in and asked how I was doing, I would try to start with the positive. Coming up with a positive often took a lot of time. It was easy to think of things that were going wrong. My life was filled with things that were wrong. To ignore that and concentrate on finding positives was the challenge, a challenge I often met head on with procrastination.

One way to avoid my problems was to sleep. I slept as much as I could. Time didn't move as slow in my sleep, and once asleep, my problems didn't exist. I would catch myself daydreaming as well. Sitting in my chair, I'd stare out the window lost in another world, a world in which I could still walk and run. A world where I could teach and live the life I wanted. Then reality would creep back in and I would fall further toward depression. I would start to feel sorry for myself with all the things I couldn't do. It seemed as if my mind would get stuck on negative. I knew I had to fight it, and I knew I needed God.

I spent a lot of time going back and forth between talking to myself and talking with God. *Come on*

Tim, you can think of something. Not everything that's happening is bad. Dear God, please help me. I'm not giving in to depression anymore. I need you. I know I can't overcome these thoughts on my own. Come on, think Tim. What's going right? I'm not sure if it's healthy to talk to yourself, but I know it's healthy to pray, and God always answered.

No matter how bad the situation seemed, there was always something positive happening. I might still be nauseous, but it was better than the day before. I would get out of bed and see if I could walk further than I had previously been able to. Maybe I could stay awake longer before I needed to take another nap. Anything I could find in my life that was a positive I tried to dwell on and tell people. I had to. If I didn't, the depression took over.

When the nurses would ask me how I was doing, I'd tell them everything that was better. I would often try to call Joan and the boys or my parents as soon as I got good news of any kind just to celebrate every little inch of progress. And I would talk to myself. Over and over I reminded myself that I was getting better and that things weren't as bad as they could have been. I was not going to let my thoughts lie to me and tell me that things were hopeless. I knew God was working and I didn't want to miss out on what he would do.

My progress, though slow at first, began to accelerate. My nausea began to dissipate and my temperature returned to normal. When Joan, Kevin, and

Eric would come for visits on Saturday and Sunday, I was able to walk out of the hospital with them and spend time at a park or even go out to eat at certain restaurants. I was again experiencing the hand of God on my life. It had yet to totally sink in, but I was beginning to understand that God had allowed the cancer into my life so he could reveal himself to me in a new way. The one thing I needed—even more than healing—was to get to know God better. [6]

After 20 days in the hospital, I was discharged on Saturday, October 5. Joan, Kevin, and Eric arrived at Froedtert around ten o'clock in the morning all set to bring me home. I had everything packed, and I was ready to go. There was just one problem. No one was free to finish the work that was necessary for me to be discharged, and it was now well into the afternoon. One of the nurses came in and informed us that I might need to stay until the next day, but then another nurse came in and told us we had to leave the room because another patient was being admitted into my room. I couldn't leave, but I couldn't stay.

Once again, the nursing staff came to our rescue. I'm not sure exactly how they pulled it off, but I do know they refused to have me leave my room without the information, training, and equipment that Joan and I would need for me to survive at home. A short time later, the necessary paperwork, prescriptions, and informational pamphlets arrived and we were free to go. I was still weak, could go from shivering to sweating almost instantly, and never knew when the nausea would hit me, but I was going home. I never felt better.

Fall 2002

To say Joan and the boys had the house clean would be an incredible understatement. The house was immaculate. My release from the hospital came with a few conditions. Number one on the list was that the house had to be as germ-free as possible. Due to my weakened immune system, it would be very easy for me to catch just about anything a germ had to offer, and at the first sign of sickness I would be back in the hospital.

In addition to the house being germ free, the food had to be thoroughly clean. Before I was allowed to eat any fruit or vegetables, they had to be washed with warm water and anti-bacterial soap. This meant no fruit or salad at restaurants and absolutely no buffets. The list of places we could go to was pretty small.

Finding completely germ-free food wasn't the only thing that kept me from getting out of the house. I wasn't allowed to be around groups of people either, and because our church is fairly large, this meant no church. This was hard on me for a number of reasons. I really wanted to go to church, and I missed hearing the message and worshiping with others. Church always had a positive impact on me, and not attending served as a weekly reminder of how sick I was.

It was also important for me to have my blood tested twice a week. This proved to be one of the biggest hurdles in me being allowed to go home when I did. We had to convince Dr. Vesole that we would be able to make the trip from Green Bay to Freodtert Hospital in Milwaukee, two (and sometimes even three) times each week. At first we weren't sure how we could make this work, but then people started stepping forward to help.

Usually Joan drove me and my sister, Ruth, watched the boys. On days Joan couldn't make the trip, Ruth would try to arrange it with work to drive me down, or my Dad would come down from Sturgeon Bay and drive me. People from church offered to watch the boys for us, and a couple of times, Pastor Dennis Nonnamacher, the Bayside Missions Pastor, drove me to Milwaukee. If we weren't sure I could get a ride during the week, Joan would take me to my brother Wally's house. I would stay with them for a few days and my sister-in-law, Dottie, would drive me to the hospital. During the two months I needed to travel to Milwaukee, I never missed an appointment.

By the middle of November, I had improved to the point that I was able to attend church, and for Thanksgiving we celebrated by traveling to Carolyn's in Kankakee, IL. I'll never forget how excited everyone was to see me. My taste buds were pretty much worthless at that point, but just being there made it one of the best meals I've ever had. We would tease that it was definitely the best meal I never tasted.

Chapter 6

Second Stem Cell Transplant

Finding A Donor

Dr. Vesole wanted me back at Froedtert as soon as possible for my second stem cell transplant. It turned out, however, that the earliest possible date would put me in the hospital for Christmas and New Years. Obviously we weren't too excited about that, and fortunately Dr. Vesole wasn't either, so we put off the second stem cell transplant for a few days. On Monday, January 6, 2003, I entered Froedtert for round two.

This time I would be receiving stem cells from my youngest brother, Joel. As soon as we knew that my life depended on whether or not I could get a stem cell transplant from one of my brothers or sisters (this took place back in September) they all immediately volunteered to be tested. None of them asked about the procedure. Would it be painful? Would they lose time at work? I'm sure they had questions, but they didn't ask. They just went in to be tested, hoping to help me live.

Only siblings were allowed to be donors and there were ten categories that each of them had to be tested for. In order to donate their stem cells for me, they had to perfectly match me in all ten categories. Ruth, Rhoda, and Wally all matched in nine categories, but failed to match all ten. This left it up to my brother Joel to see if I was going to get the second stem cell transplant I needed.

Joel was living in South Carolina and he was tested at a local hospital near where he lived. We then had to wait for his test to make it to Milwaukee for analysis. The wait was excruciating, but finally the news came. Joel was a perfect match in all ten categories! I would get the second stem cell transplant.

It was important to get stem cells from a donor in order to rebuild my platelets, along with my red and white blood cell count. The hope was that Joel's stem cells would, upon entering my body, form cancer-free bone marrow, and that this new bone marrow would produce a new immune system strong enough to destroy cancer cells. (My old immune system had stopped recognizing cancer cells as something to destroy.)

As improbable and impossible as this all sounds, the hardest part was yet to come. My old immune system, while weak, was still at work and would recognize Joel's stem cells as a foreign substance and try to destroy them. Joel's stem cells needed time to grow in my body, form bone marrow, and begin to produce white blood cells that would attack and overpower my old, deficient immune system instead. For however long it took, I was going to have two immune systems in my body, fighting for supremacy. In order for me to live, Joel's stem cells had to be the victors.

Joel Comes to Town

Joel arrived in Milwaukee on Tuesday, January 7 and immediately started the preparations to donate stem cells. It was a fun time for both of us as Joel would come to my hospital room whenever he could. We watched old reruns on TV, played games, talked, and to the degree that I could, we goofed off as much as possible. I remember laughing a lot when Joel was there. If laughter is the best medicine, Joel was a pharmaceutical company.

After donating his stem cells, Joel stayed for one extra day to make sure he was alright and then had to head home. One of the hardest moments of my life was saying goodbye. How do you thank someone for giving you the opportunity to live? He kept saying it was nothing, and maybe to him it was, but to me it was the chance to see my boys grow up, to grow old with Joan, to see my grandkids, to teach again. His "little thing" as he called it, was my everything. I'm alive today because he cared enough to give for me.

<u>After The Transplant</u>

As soon as I finished going through all the pre-transplant requirements expected of me, and every-thing with Joel checked out, I received Joel's stem cells. I wasn't sure what to expect. I had been warned that this transplant would probably be harder than the first one, and that my hospital stay could be 30 days or longer. I was told to once again expect nausea, loss of the ability to taste, elevated temperature, and loss of energy. In addition, the nurses constantly checked for mouth sores. While I never had mouth sores, everything else happened.

For me, the worst part was the nausea. I constantly felt nauseous, but very seldom threw up. I would actually hope to throw up, thinking that doing so might bring some relief. As funny as it sounds now, after a few days I did find some relief. One morning I was particularly miserable. The nausea was unbear-able. I was just lying in bed, taking deep breaths, and trying hard not to move, when I burped. It wasn't a polite little burp either. If you go back and check the seismological record for that day in Milwaukee, I'm sure you'll find a reading for that morning. And then

I felt fine. From then on, whenever I felt nauseous, I did everything I could to burp, and the nausea would go away. Once I made my great medical discovery, the nausea wasn't as bad. Every once in a while it would prove to be a day-long problem, but not like it had been. I'm not sure doctors anywhere would recommend burping to handle the nausea associated with stem cell transplants, and I have no idea why it helped. I'm just glad it did.

My progress was almost unbelievable, and by the thirteenth day I was allowed to leave the hospital. I wasn't allowed to go home to Green Bay, but my brother Wally and his family opened up their home in Milwaukee to me and I stayed with them. Every morning that first week, one of them would drive me to the Oncology Clinic at Froedtert and I'd have my blood tested along with a very basic physical. At the end of the first week, Dr. Vesole decided that I could go home for the weekend.

Rather than calling home to tell everyone the good news, my sister-in-law, Dottie, decided to drive me home and make it a big surprise. I'll never forget walking in the door. Everyone went nuts, including our dog, Tipper. It felt so good to be at home, sitting in my own recliner in our own living room and getting to sleep in my own bed. Everything seemed surreal. I just had my second stem cell transplant and here I was only three weeks later at home for the weekend. I couldn't see anyone outside of the family, and I was under strict orders, once again, that if anyone showed even the slightest sign of being sick, I was to leave immediately. Fortunately that weekend everyone was healthy, but that was about to change.

Fragile Condition

Monday morning I had to be at the Bone Marrow Transplant Clinic (BMT) by eight o'clock in the morning, so I drove back to Wally's house in Milwaukee Sunday night. Having my own vehicle again was fantastic. I didn't feel like such a burden to my brother's family. I know they didn't look at me as a burden, and I will forever be grateful to them and admire them for that, but it really gave me a feeling of getting better when I was able to take myself to the clinic.

That Thursday, my thankfulness for having my own vehicle in Milwaukee turned into necessity. When I got up in the morning, Dottie informed me that one of their kids had a scratchy throat. She wasn't sure it would turn into anything, but wanted me to be aware of it so we could keep an eye on the situation. My appointment with the clinic wasn't until later that day, so I decided it would be wise to call them and find out at what point I would need to leave.

It was then that I was hit right between the eyes with how fragile my condition really was. The nurse I was talking with didn't even let me finish my conversation. She ordered me out of the house immediately. I tried to talk with her, but she insisted I grab my coat and get out of the house right away. The problem was, I had no idea where to go. She told me to go sit in the car and call her on the cell phone. Fortunately, the temperature was above freezing. The previous days had been below zero and I wouldn't have been able to sit in the car until it warmed up.

I went right out to our mini-van, started the engine, got the heater set, and called the clinic back. They reminded me that my immune system was almost non-existent. The drugs I was taking to strengthen my new immune system were also reducing my old immune system. I had two immune systems in me slugging it out for superiority, but neither one was really capable at that time of stopping anything. For the time being, I realistically had no immune system.

Dottie came out to the van and we decided that the best thing would be for her to pack up my things and bring them out to me. (I don't think anyone was ever more blessed with sister-in-laws than me.) Once she brought everything out, we talked for a few moments, and then I had to take off. It was so hard to see their three kids, Abbey, Amanda, and Zach, in the window waving goodbye. They had opened their home to me, put up with all the inconveniences I caused them, prayed with me and for me, and helped me in every way possible, and now I was leaving without even saying thank you. It seemed so wrong to leave that way, but I knew I had to.

I drove around for a little while and then decided to go to the clinic and wait for my appointment. When the time came, Dr. Vesole and I talked about what to do next. Things were going really well for me and Dr. Vesole decided I could have my blood tested with Dr. Jaslowski in Green Bay and drive to Milwaukee once a week to see him, if I wanted to go home for good. *If* I wanted to go home to stay? This was a question for which only one word could really convey my complete and total answer. "Duh!"

As soon as I left the BMT unit, I called Joan to give her the good news. I was on my way home and home I stayed—that is, until three days later when Eric started to show signs of a cold. I called Froedtert and it was decided that the best place for me to go would be my parents' house in Sturgeon Bay. It was another hour north of Green Bay, but it would be the best place for me to stay because my parents never get sick. Or I should say they never *got* sick. Now, though, they did.

We laugh about it now, but at the time it was no laughing matter. There was no place safe for me to go. It looked like I would be going back to the hospital. It was just too dangerous for me to live with other people, and in a BMT room I would be safe. Of course, the insurance company was less than thrilled with this arrangement. Putting me back in the hospital would not be cheap, so they came up with another solution. They would put me up in a motel near the hospital in Milwaukee. After some discussions between the people at Froedtrert and the insurance company, a decision was made as to where I could stay, so I moved into my motel room and stayed there for three weeks.

All Alone

Once again, I received strict orders to stay away from people, so I was given a room at the end of the hallway to keep me separated from the majority of those staying in the motel. This worked out great as far as keeping me away from people, but it was horrible when it came to breakfast. The motel had a nice breakfast, but it was served near the front desk. The only way for me to get it was to walk there, so I would grab my cane and off I'd go.

After a couple of days, I started to keep track of how much time it took me to walk to breakfast each morning. Depending on how my leg felt and how much energy I had, it was anywhere from three to five minutes, but I made it. Then I was usually presented with a new problem. Other guests would be in the breakfast area and my orders were to eat alone, so I would grab whatever I could hold in one hand and using my cane with the other, start back down the hallway to my room. Once in my room,

I'd set my items down and head back to the front again to get something to drink.

At first, because I could only hold things in one hand, it would take four trips to the front to get breakfast, but with practice I got it down to three. The first trip I'd get a bowl of cereal, the second trip I'd get a muffin or a piece of toast, and with the third trip I'd get milk and orange juice. To get the milk and orange juice in one hand, I would fill up the cups, put my index finger in one and my thumb in the other, pinch the two cups together, and start down the hallway. A couple times I dropped the cups and had to go back to the front desk, let them know I spilled the drinks, and then do it all over again.

Once again, I had no idea the way people were watching me. I was just living with tunnel vision. I would walk down the hallway, and in my mind I'd be yelling at the cancer the whole way down the hallway. *I'm not dead and I'm still moving. You want to take me, you're going to have to work for it. I'm not giving in.* I can't tell you how many times that thought went through my head. *I'm not giving in.*

Often I would get halfway down the hallway and get scared. What if I couldn't get back to my room? My leg hurt, I was losing energy, and there were no nurses here to help me. What if I fell? How would I get up? I'd feel the fear begin to grip me and, at times, grab me to the point that I would start shaking. What if I couldn't get back to my room? Right about then I would hear in my thoughts, *Are you giving in?* Sometimes it took awhile, but in each case I answered *No!* and kept moving forward.

I learned a big lesson from this. Often the greatest success we can have is to keep moving. Don't give in. Keep moving forward. Down the hallway I'd go, thinking about the verse, "I can do all things through Christ who strengthens me." [7] I came to realize that the verse does not say "I can do all things right away." *Eventually* was not one of my favorite words. I wanted it now. But given the choice between eventually and not at all, eventually doesn't seem so bad.

Over time, I became aware that the things I treasure most are the things that came eventually. Things that came with a price. Things that I had to struggle for. Things that were born of determination. Things that pushed me beyond what I thought were my limits. These are the things that God uses to show us who we are in Him. If I let Him, these are the things God will use to prove who He is. These are the things God will use, in His time, to prove that "all things are possible for those who believe"[8] and keep on believing, and keep on believing, and keep on and on and on.

Too often I would believe, but if the answer I wanted didn't come right away, I got angry, confused, and discouraged. I knew that had to change, and God evidently really wanted me to change. We serve a very persistent God. I might give up, but He never does. I don't necessarily think God kept working on me because He had some incredible faith in my ability to change, but rather He had faith in His ability to change me. I was ready for all this to end. God wasn't. He won.

Chapter 7

Summer 2003

God, Why?

I was gaining weight—lots of weight. My body was filling up with fluids and nothing the doctors did seemed to have any effect. By August of 2003, I had grown to almost 400 pounds. The doctors had never seen this reaction from anyone with multiple myeloma before and weren't sure what was causing it or what to do. The skin was stretched tight across my entire body, making any movement so painful that I just quit moving. As much as possible, I sat in a chair and read or watched TV, trying not to move.

Where was God? I knew God could heal me. Look at what He'd already done. So why wasn't He healing me? What had changed? When God had healed me, I didn't really think He would. Now that I trusted God and believed Him for healing, nothing was happening. My mind was a blur. Why wasn't God healing me?

I now completely understand the Children of Israel in the desert with Moses. In the past, I was always confused by the Israelites. How could they watch God perform an incredible miracle and then just a short time later start complaining again? Now I understood. I was just like them.

Once God performs an incredible miracle in your life, you begin to expect it all the time. Once you've experienced firsthand the power of God working in your own life, there is no longer any doubt in your mind as to what God can do. So the next time a big problem comes into your life, you expect God to miraculously take care of it again. You know beyond any shadow of a doubt that He can, so you pray and expect it to happen. When the miracle doesn't instantly come, you get confused. You know God is capable of instantly changing things, so why doesn't He. At that moment, it's very easy to come to a very troubling conclusion: God could help, but won't. It was proving to be harder to go through suffering now after God had healed me than before.

Before God healed my back and did absolutely incredible things with my leg, I wasn't completely sure of God's healing powers. But now I knew. I had felt his power flow through me. Before my healing, I believed God could heal, but I really wasn't sure he would do it for me. Now I knew he would. Which left one question. Why wasn't God healing me now? At first I got angry and then fell into a deep depression. People told me there was sin in my life that I wasn't facing up to and that God was allowing this into my life because of it. Others told me I had a demon in me, or that it was because I didn't have enough seaweed or kelp in my diet. I took all these things to the Lord in prayer and begged for His guidance.

I repented of everything I could think of, and pleaded with God to show me the sin in my life that was causing this. No matter how I pleaded, no matter how I cried, no matter how I prayed, I got nothing. My only answer was the intense, constant pain that grew worse every day. Where was God? What kind of cruel God would allow this into my life?

Little by little, I began to believe that I had done something so bad that God was trying to make me suffer before he killed me. In my confusion and depression, I would beg God to show me what I had done so that I could apologize. Often I would just lie in bed, my body completely engulfed in pain, and just cry over and over "God I'm sorry, I'm sorry. Whatever I did, God, I'm sorry." My body just got worse and the pain grew more severe.

One night I complained to Joan that I just wanted it all to end. I was tired of the pain and tired of trying to figure out what was wrong. Joan tried to encourage me and added that I should consider whether this might be a Job experience. [9] I replied that I thought Job was just a toy. God called Satan's attention to Job just so they could play with him. As an afterthought, I added that maybe this *was* a Job experience. Satan comes to God and says, "Let me do this to Tim," and God says, "Fine, go ahead." Then Satan comes back and says, "Let me add this to Tim," and God says, "Fine, go ahead." Maybe that's what it was after all. I was just a toy. Right away, I told Joan that I didn't really believe that to be true, but it was what I was feeling.

God Is Bigger

The next morning, I decided to watch the Joyce Meyers television program. In the past, I watched Joyce Meyers fairly regularly, but as I grew angry and confused with God, I stopped watching. That particular morning, her husband Dave Meyers talked about his migraine headaches and how debilitating they had been. Finally, one day he decided to stop concentrating on how big the migraine was and start focusing instead on how much bigger God was. He testified that at first nothing changed, but he refused to let the migraines stop him. He forced himself to keep going and concentrate on how much bigger God was than the migraine, and over a period of time, the migraines stopped. That's when I realized that I needed to change my perspective.

Instead of only praying for God to heal me, I needed to pray and believe that God could make me happy and content just the way I was, that He was bigger than the problems I faced, and that He could give me a rich, rewarding, joy-filled life even if my circumstances never changed. God's answer this time wasn't to give my body a quick healing, it was to empower me to overcome.

I still vividly remember that moment when, as I was sitting in our recliner I told God that if he never healed me I would love Him and serve Him. I was no longer going to concentrate on how big my problems were, but rather on how much bigger He was than my problems. I believed He loved me, that He would never leave me, and that He could and would make all things work together for good, even if my circumstances never changed.

In my body, nothing changed. Every square inch of flesh continued to hurt excessively; but I was happy, instantly happy. Tears welled up in my eyes, but this time in joy, relief, and absolute bewilderment that I could experience such a high without any change in my circumstance. This had to be God. Where else would this have come from? I knew it wasn't me. All I could muster up on my own had been confusion and depression, and this definitely wasn't depression. I had never experienced peace like this. I just knew everything would be okay. Even if nothing physically changed, everything would be okay.

I Will Serve God!

My thoughts tried to bring me down. Over the next couple of days, questions would pop into my head. *What kind of a God would leave you this way? You're still in pain, why won't God heal you? You're useless to people the way you are. What kind of a father are you now? What kind of a husband are you now? What kind of Christian witness are you now? Why serve God if He's going to leave you in this kind of pain?*

My parents came to our house and I told them what had happened. I believed I was getting to know God in a way I would never otherwise have had the chance to know Him. But I also told them about the nagging doubts and questions that wouldn't completely go away. Just as they had done for as long as I can remember, they said, "Let's pray about it and see what God does."

As my parents prayed, the questions in my mind began to grow in intensity, questions about God's love for me. *Why serve God if this is what you get? Why serve God if he's going to leave you this way?* Over and over the questions throbbed in my mind. I couldn't seem to think. My Dad was five feet away from me, and I knew he was praying, but I couldn't hear him. The voices just grew louder and louder. *Why serve God? Why serve God?*

There must have been a break in my thoughts, because I heard Dad say, "Tim you need to pray," and right then my thoughts commanded me *Leave God!* In anger, I formed a fist, flung it in the air, and yelled "THAT'S ENOUGH. I WILL NOT LEAVE GOD. I WILL SERVE GOD!" It wasn't a very eloquent prayer, but it was all I could muster. It was from the heart and it had an immediate effect.

New thoughts began to flood my mind, thoughts of thankfulness to God for loving me, thoughts of submission to God no matter what might happen, and thoughts of how big God was and how much I wanted to serve Him. There had been many times in the past in which I had these thoughts, but they never flowed this freely. These thoughts were confident, and most amazingly to me, they flowed uninhibited. No doubts and no questions rose up to stand in the way.

I sat there and enjoyed the moment. To me, this seemed a bigger miracle than the healing of my back. It was bigger than walking on a leg with a jagged femur and a disintegrating hip. This was God touching me—not to heal me, but just to be close to me. I was beginning to understand what God had been trying to teach me all along. Through the cancer I was learning, in a unique and powerful way, how much God loved me, that He had a plan for my life, that He is bigger than any problem I will ever face, and that by faith and trust in God I can experience peace and joy in any situation. My problem was God's opportunity to reveal Himself to me and build a personal relationship with me.

Positive, powerful, enlightening thoughts kept flowing. Scriptures that had confused me for years were now making sense, such as how the apostles could praise and thank God for counting them "worthy to suffer."[10] What it meant to be "more than a conqueror,"[11] just as God was liberating me, I was to be used by God to liberate others. I was meant to be more than a conqueror. I was meant to be a liberator, and to allow God to use me to bring this same freedom to others.

I was really beginning to understand. I was created to be close to God! When I was born, God's plan wasn't to help me make it through an awful life here on earth and then be close to Him someday in heaven. He wants to be close to me now. He wants me to know Him now.

Now is a wonderful time. There are things I can learn about God and myself now that I won't be able to learn in heaven. Now, as I face life's problems, I have the opportunity to see how much bigger God is than the problems. Now, as problems come up, I have the most meaningful opportunity that I may have for all of eternity to let God know how much I love him. Now, I can let God know that no problem will get me to leave him. Now, I can build a reputation that may last for all eternity as an overcomer through faith in God. Now, I can experience what it is like to be used by God under difficult and even horrible circumstances. Now, I can get to know and grow close to God. I don't have to wait for heaven.

For the first time in my life, I was free. The new thoughts could flow because I was free of the fear and control the old thoughts had held over me. Every time those old thoughts come back now, (and they do come back), I can control them. They no longer have power over me. I no longer believe God loves me—I know it. I no longer believe He's bigger than my problems—I know it. I know he will work all things together for good. I know he has a plan for me. I know he won't leave me, [12] and I know I'm not leaving Him.

My outward circumstances hadn't changed, but it no longer mattered to me. My prayer now was *God I trust you and if you want me to spend the rest of my life this way, I know that's what's best for me.* I realized how fear had controlled my life, fear of making mistakes, fear of not being the husband and father I thought I should be, fear of poor health, fear of financial problems, and fear of problems period.

Now I realized I needed only one thing in my life: a desire to please God. I don't need to fear mistakes; I can't possibly make a mistake big enough that God can't straighten it out. As a husband and father, my wife and sons were better off with me in my current condition (if that was in the will of God) than in perfect health out of the will of God. Trying to first be what I thought they needed me to be was wrong. I needed to please God first and allow Him to make me the husband and father He wanted me to be. I needed to let Him love my wife and sons through me. As to fear of finances—If God didn't supply it, I didn't need it; if I needed it, God would supply it.

Problems were no longer a thing to fear. As God opened my understanding, it became clear to me that all problems, no matter how big or small, are opportunities for God. They are opportunities for God to show me where I've gone wrong, or who I am when I don't completely trust him, opportunities for him to show me how much bigger he is than any problem I will ever face, and opportunities to show me that a life intertwined with His is much better than a life lived on my own.

For nine years I had the privilege of working side by side with Luther Appel, Director of Bands at Bay Port High School in Green Bay. He's a phenomenal director whose bands have been recognized time and again as being among the best in the state, and even the nation. One of the things Luther would say to his students was now ringing through my ears. Whenever the students would get tired of the hard work it takes to achieve excellence, Luther would remind them, "I never said it would be easy, I just said it would be worth it." That perfectly describes building a close, deep, personal relationship with God. It won't be easy, but it is definitely worth it.

Chapter 8

Is Surgery Possible?

About two weeks after this experience, Dr. Jaslowski was able to piece together the cause of my fluid build-up and placed me on medication that began to help immediately. One of the concerns with the fluid build-up had been how it would affect my chances for getting a new hip and femur. It was impossible for Dr. Hackbarth to do replacement surgery with all that fluid in my body. The surgery would just be too hard to perform. Even if he could successfully perform the surgery, the massive amounts of fluid I had in me guaranteed that I would develop serious and life-threatening infections. However now that I was losing fluid and my weight was going down, it was again possible to think about the surgery. But I needed to lose more fluid.

Day by day, the fluid slowly drained from my body and as it did, most of my pain began to subside. That is, except for my left leg. God seemed to be pulling His miraculous hand off my leg, which had once again decreased in length, and the pain in my leg was steadily increasing, making it harder for me to walk with just the aid of the cane. More and more I was finding I needed to use the walker to get around, and at times the pain was so bad I just didn't move or I needed a wheelchair. It was becoming obvious that without surgery to replace my hip and femur, I would soon be unable to walk at all.

Joan and I arranged to meet with Dr. Hackbarth at Froedtert Hospital at the end of September. When the day came, I first headed to the x-ray unit to have x-rays taken of my left leg. Once this was completed, we headed back to the orthopedics area and waited a short time for Dr. Hackbarth. He showed us the x-rays and explained all the problems that would or could occur for me with surgery, and informed us that his decision was to not do the surgery. There wasn't enough bone left in my leg to tie a replacement hip and femur into and there was just too much fluid yet. Even if there was a way for someone in my condition to have their hip and femur replaced, the chance that I'd get a life-threatening infection was way too high. We knew what this ultimately meant. There was a very strong possibility that I would never have the surgery. I needed to prepare to spend the rest of my life in a wheelchair.

Gone was any hope of one day being able to play football with my sons again. I would never get to pitch to them and work on their hitting. The walks Joan and I used to go on together were now forever a thing of the past, and our dream of going hiking as a family with Kevin and Eric was over. Those things were never going to happen. My life was going to be lived in a wheelchair.

I knew I should turn this over to God and trust Him with this, but I couldn't. My prayers became desperate attempts to talk God into healing my leg the way He had healed my back. Over and over I explained to God how much glory he'd receive from healing me. Deep inside, though, I knew that I wasn't praying nearly as much for God's glory as for my own desire to walk. I didn't want to be in a wheelchair! What could I do in a wheelchair other than be a burden to people? (I know now how ridiculous these thoughts really were, but that's the state of mind I was in.)

I went round and round with God. I didn't want to fall into depression again, but how could I be happy in a wheelchair. I kept reminding myself that God was bigger than this problem and that He was not sitting in heaven completely stumped by how to handle my situation. God had a plan and He knew what He wanted to do. My Dad's words rang in my ears. "It's not whether God is with you Tim, but whether you stay with God. God already knows how this will turn out and if you trust Him, it will work out for good." I believed that was true if God healed me, but how could that be true if He left me in a wheelchair? What good could come from me being in a wheelchair? I couldn't figure it out.

Little by little I began to understand that there was no need for me to figure it out. There was, however, a need for me to trust God. I was asking God *why* in anger, frustration, and depression. It was ok to ask *why*, but He wanted me to ask with an open mind ready to receive the blessing of His closeness no matter what the answer.

I still remember bowing my head as I sat in our living room, committing my future to the will of the Lord. My prayer was, *Lord I trust You. I willingly accept whatever You do with my life. I know You can heal me at any moment. All it would take is a word from You and I'd have a brand new leg. Lord I also believe that You are big enough to make me the happiest person who's ever been in a wheelchair and that either way You can be glorified. Lord, You do Your will and I trust You that You will work all this out for good for me, Joan, Kevin, and Eric.*

There were no fireworks. Angels didn't surround me singing the "Hallelujah Chorus." I didn't suddenly receive a complete healing and run across the room. Instead I experienced one of the biggest gifts God gives—a real sense of peace and contentment. I knew that no matter what happened, we were going to be okay. If I were to spend the rest of my life in a wheelchair, that would be just fine.

I began to understand how foolish I had been for thinking I had to walk to be happy. I had so many preconceived notions of what I needed to be happy, and most of them were wrong. My life was not over, and I wasn't worthless just because my legs didn't work right. I was as happy now in the wheelchair as I had ever been in my life. I still had no idea what God was up to, but I knew it would be good.

Right before Thanksgiving, Dr. Hackbarth's office called to see how we were doing. As we talked, they informed us that he really hadn't given up on replacing my hip and femur. Without telling us, he had been calling other surgeons to try to come up with a way to perform the surgery. They went on to say that he now thought he could overcome the problems involved and was wondering if we could come back to Froedtert on January 21 for the surgery. Joan and I prayed about it for about half a second and said, "Yes!"

I was stunned. I might really get to walk again. I would probably need the walker or cane the rest of my life, but at least I would be out of the wheelchair. That Christmas was enjoyable, but hard. The enjoyable part was obvious. I was alive and there was a good chance I would get out of the wheelchair. The hard part was waiting. Now that I knew surgery was possible, I wanted it as soon as I could.

Chapter 9

Surgery

On January 21, Joan and I got up at four o'clock in the morning and headed to Milwaukee. Dr. Hackbarth wanted us there by seven o'clock in the morning, and there was no way we were going to be late. We checked in, were given a beeper to let us know when everything was set, and went to the family waiting room. It took about an hour, but finally our beeper went off, and we were directed to a small prep room.

The room was about eight feet wide and ten feet long with medical shelves and drawers along the back wall. Right in the middle of the room was a hospital bed. A small TV hanging from the ceiling on an adjustable arm was right next to it. On the other side of the bed was a chair. The nurses had some questions for Joan, so while they were out of the room, I changed into a hospital gown and worked my way onto the bed.

When Joan got back to the room, she told me that there was a mix-up with some paperwork and that we would have to wait for awhile. Some of the papers they needed were missing and they couldn't start without them. They knew where they could get copies, so it was just a matter of waiting. I hate that word *waiting*, but it doesn't seem to bother God, so we waited.

Finally one of the nurses came back in and said they could get started. The first thing they needed to do was insert the needle for the IV. The nurse looked at my wrist and forearm, but couldn't find a vein. She called for another nurse and together they tried to find a spot where they could get the IV needle into a vein, but all their attempts were futile. I still had too much fluid in my body and the needle couldn't reach through it to enter the vein. They refused to give up though since giving up meant I couldn't have the surgery. I needed the IV.

After about 30 minutes of trying, the nurses left to go get the most experienced nurse on the staff to see if she could get the IV needle inserted. While they were out of the room, Joan and I prayed. It just didn't seem possible that God would have opened up the doors to surgery only for me to have them slammed shut in my face now.

In a few minutes, all three nurses came back into the room. The third nurse took the IV needle and began to work on my arm. She had me do various things in an attempt to make the veins easier to find, but no matter what she tried, she couldn't find a vein to use either. She was extremely determined and kept saying "we're not giving up on that surgery yet," and then it happened. Blood began to flow through the needle in a very good blood draw. The IV could be hooked up and the surgery could get started.

A short time later I entered the operating room. The staff made one last check to make sure they were operating on the correct leg and then off to sleep I went. They had prepared us for a four hour surgery, so when four hours passed with no word on how I was doing, Joan began to get worried. At seven hours, Dr. Hackbarth came and told Joan they were closing up and that I had stopped breathing twice. Everything else had gone well, but they had to put me on a ventilator and would keep me in the ICU until they were sure I could breathe on my own.

What's Happening? I Can't Move!

The first thing I remember after surgery was people calling my name and speaking to me. I kept trying to understand them, but nothing made sense. I was still pretty groggy. I knew the voices were off to my side, so I tried to move my head in that direction, but my head wouldn't move. Little by little I started to understand the voices, but when I tried to speak, nothing would come out.

I was really confused. I didn't know where I was. I tried desperately to move, but nothing worked. I couldn't move my head, my arms, my legs, my feet, my hands, nothing. I started to panic. Nothing made sense. I could hear now, but I couldn't answer. My mouth wouldn't move. On my whole body, the only thing I had control over to move were my eyelids. Fear gripped me. Was I paralyzed? I didn't know.

Joan and my brother, Wally, were next to my bed and by rolling my eyes to the right I could see them. Next to them was a woman I didn't recognize. Joan and Wally were telling me everything would be okay, but they both looked really worried as the woman next to them began to explain what was happening. I remember her saying that I was in the Intensive Care Unit. I had stopped breathing during the operation and had to be revived, and when it happened a second time, they put me on a ventilator. They didn't know why I had stopped breathing and were very concerned that it would happen again. The reason I couldn't speak was that the tube from the breathing machine had been inserted down my throat.

Doctor Hackbarth and the medical staff were very concerned that I might panic at some point and try to pull my tube out, or that by rolling around I might inadvertently move the breathing tube. For that reason, along with the need to keep my hip totally still, I was completely tied down. They needed to make sure I couldn't move and put straps across my stomach, chest, thighs, calves, feet, arms and hands. In addition, my head was being held in place by a vice. Until the medical staff knew I could breathe on my own, the number one priority was to keep the breathing tube in place, and to guarantee that I absolutely did not move.

I was trapped. I wanted to move, make a sound, somehow prove to myself I was alive! I really wasn't sure. Over and over I thought *God can hear me. God can hear me. Calm down. God can hear me. Dear God, I can't talk. I can't move. Please, dear God, you've got to hear me.* I kept thinking, *don't panic. Analyze this. What did they tell you? What's going on?*

I tried to make sense of what was happening. It couldn't be as bad as it seemed, but it was. I was completely immobile, with no ability to communicate with anyone. I had a breathing tube in my mouth and down my throat, an IV was feeding me, and I couldn't even go to the bathroom on my own. Machines and drugs were taking care of that also. I could move my eyes and think. That was it. And my thoughts were quickly becoming my enemy.

I'm Not Dying Here!

The nurse left the room, leaving me alone with Joan and Wally. They did their best to keep my spirits up, but that was a hard task to do while dealing with their own fears for me. There was a monitor that gauged how much air was moving through my breathing tube, and Joan was keeping a very close eye on it. Moisture would build up inside the tube and block the flow of air into my lungs. When the air movement dropped down to a certain level, the nurse would come in and suction the water out of the tube. I had no way of letting anyone know if I was gagging on the moisture, so I was completely dependent on the accuracy of the monitor and on someone being present to read it.

I could hear Joan tell Wally that the readings were getting pretty low and that someone should come and suction my tube out. I could hear Wally walk out into the hallway and come back, and then I listened as he told Joan that no one was around. I was beginning to have trouble breathing and was hoping that one of the nurses would come soon. Listening to Joan and Wally, I could tell that their level of concern was rising as they kept checking the hallway to see if anyone was coming.

I was now really struggling to breathe. I couldn't get air. My lungs were starting to hurt. I yelled, but didn't make a sound. All I could hear was gurgling coming from my tube. My lungs were burning. I couldn't breathe. There was no air. I rolled my eyes back and forth trying to find someone, but no one was within sight. I thought *I'm not dying here* and tried harder to get air, but got nothing.

I could now hear Joan and Wally asking for help and Wally kept saying, "Someone's going to come, Tim, keep breathing. Someone's going to come." Joan headed down the hallway looking for help. I wasn't going to die this way, and I fought with all I had, but I had no choice. I couldn't get any air in my lungs. I remember thinking, *Okay Lord, then here I come*, and right at that moment, someone suctioned out my tube and my lungs filled with air.

My eyes searched for Joan and I found her, standing as close to me as she could while the nurse worked. I wanted to hold her, to thank her, to tell her how much I loved her, but I couldn't do a thing. She had just saved my life and I couldn't do a thing. I rolled my eyes searching for Wally and I found him standing close to Joan. He kept saying "you're going to be alright Tim. You're going to be alright," and I loved hearing him say it. I believed it when he said it. I wanted him to know how much he meant to me and all I could do was look at them and blink my eyes.

When the nurse finished, I heard her say words that tore my heart out. "You'll have to leave now. Visiting hours are over." She was making Joan and Wally leave and there was nothing I could do to stop it. I didn't want them to leave. I desperately wanted them to stay, but I could do nothing. Joan and Wally argued with the nurse, but to no avail. Rules were rules and they would have to leave. Joan was mad and wanted to know if what had just happened could happen again. At that point I could hear a man say, "don't worry, I'll watch over him." I couldn't see him, but a sense of peace fell over me. He told Joan that he would move his desk right outside my room so he could keep a constant eye on the monitor.

Joan, still arguing to stay, came back into the room. I could feel both Joan and Wally touch me as they said goodbye. Then they were leaving. I could hear them in the hallway, still reminding the nurses to watch me, and then they were gone. I was alone. I felt as if everything in life had been taken away from me. I couldn't walk. I couldn't even move or talk. I needed a machine to breathe, eat, and go to the bathroom. I was tied down with my head in some kind of vice, and now I was alone. All I had was my eyes and what little I could see. At first I lay in bed waiting for God to take that from me as well.

Communicating

Loneliness began to envelop me when the nurse stuck his head in the room. "Tim, I was serious about setting up my desk right here outside your room. I'm going to do that right now." I could hear screeching and scraping in the hallway, getting closer and closer to my room, and then it stopped right outside my door. He came into the room and said "Tim, I want you to look down across your body toward your feet. If you can see the door I want you to quickly blink your eyes." By rolling my eyes down toward my nose I could make out the door, so I started to blink my eyes. I was communicating!

He asked me if I could see the big window next to the door, and into the hallway. I quickly blinked my eyes over and over. He told me he was going to go sit down and wanted to know if I could see him while he was sitting where he would be working just outside my room. He went out and sat down. I rolled my eyes as low as I could and I could indeed see him. He came back in and again I blinked my eyes. He told me that he would stay there all night and that if he had to leave, he would tell me before leaving, and that he would never be gone for long.

He stayed true to his word all night. To this day I wonder if he was an angel. How did he know exactly what I was thinking? How was he able to move his work to that spot where I could see him? Maybe he was a nurse and wasn't an angel at all. Maybe angels are nurses. Most likely, the vast majority of nurses are just people who have learned how to do a great angel imitation. When I get to heaven though, if I learn he was an angel, I won't be at all surprised.

Along with the loneliness, I was fighting boredom, and it's amazing how much your muscles ache when you can't move them. I closed my eyes with the hope that I would fall asleep and wake up when this was all over, but I had no such luck. I was wide awake, with nothing to do but stare at the ceiling.

Accept or Reject God

Anger started to creep into my mind, but I definitely didn't want to go there. I thought of all the things I'd been through in the past two years, and how God had proven Himself to me. He had never and would never reject me. He had never and would never leave me. Of this I was now sure. I was also sure that He was with me now. Once again, the question wasn't would God be there for me, but would I stay with God? I had a decision to make; was I going to reject God or accept Him?

I thought back to all the times I had grown depressed, angry, and discouraged with whatever I was facing before accepting God's will in the situation, and how He had always proven Himself to be bigger than anything I faced. The TV show with Dave Meyers began to play over and over in my mind. *God is bigger. God is bigger. Don't think about how big the problem is; think about how much bigger God is.* These words raced through my head and I could feel an excitement rising up inside of me.

I remember praying, *God this is it. This is a test for both of us isn't it? You've proven time and again that nothing can separate me from Your love and this is my chance to prove that nothing can separate You from my love. Lord, death would be better than this, but I know I'm not going to die. The question is, am I willing to serve You, am I willing to praise You, am I willing to thank You for what's happening to me right now? Dear God, it's so hard, but I want to get this one right.* Over and over I thought the words, *God I know You are bigger and I thank You for this chance to prove I love You.* Each time I prayed, the peace and excitement within me would grow.

I know God exists. Not because of some great archeological discovery or scientific proof, but because His Spirit overwhelmed me. For me to deny God's existence, I'd have to forget or deny what happened to me that night. The more I accepted Him the more He accepted me into Himself. The joy and peace I felt as I lay there, tied down to that hospital bed, I can only describe as pure enjoyment. God took me in the hell I was going through, and allowed me to experience heaven.

I thought about the people trying to get me to believe that God wants me to be rich, healthy, and powerful, or those that told me I had a demon, or that I must have sin in my life that God was punishing me for. I can honestly say that as the night wore on, if someone had given me a choice between having perfect health and a mansion in Hawaii, or staying right where I was, I would have chosen to stay right where I was.

I can also honestly say that I would gladly live that night again. Because of that night, I grew to understand many things about God and myself. Number one is that every problem is an opportunity for me to prove I love God. I'm not perfect in this by any means, but I am trying to face every problem in my life now by first declaring to all the hosts of heaven that this problem is not enough to get me to leave and reject Him. The problems Jesus faced on earth—including torture and the cross—were not enough to get Him to stop loving me, give up on me, or reject me, so how could I face Him, knowing I had rejected Him because of the problems I had to face.

Every problem is God's opportunity to find out how deep my love for Him is. Every problem is God's opportunity to reveal Himself to me and through me, if I let Him. Every problem is an opportunity for me to get to know the God who created the universe. Never again will I seek after all my old preconceived notions of happiness before knowing Him. I'm cured of that. My sickness, my cancer, was my cure.

At some point during the night I realized I could see the top half of the clock on the wall to my left. When the second hand would reach the top, I'd look away and not look back at the clock until I thought exactly one minute had gone by. I kept trying to see how close to exactly one minute I could get each time I looked up. When I got pretty good at that I'd try for two minutes.

With everything that was going on inside of me, just counting seconds seemed like a real waste of time, so I decided to pray for people in addition to counting seconds. This seemed to provide the challenge my mind needed. To try to sincerely pray for people and try to keep track of how many seconds went by was hard, but I eventually got pretty good at it, so I upped the ante. I decided to see how many people I could pray for each minute. So now I was counting people and seconds while trying to pray sincerely, and I was really concerned that I be praying sincerely. I remember laughing inside when I thought about someone telling me that somehow praying in the situation I was in could be anything but sincere. So I quit worrying about being sincere and just went on praying.

I have no idea how many people I prayed for that night, or how many times I prayed, but there's a very good chance that if I know you, or of you, that I prayed and/or thought about you that night. It might not sound like much. It might even sound ridiculous, but I was enjoying myself. Don't tell me there's no God. He spent the night with me.

I Can Breathe

Sometime the next morning, the nurse came in with a breathing test contraption. I'm sure it has an official name, but to me it looked like a contraption. It had a small, plastic tube that I was to blow into. At the other end of the plastic tube was a Plexiglas tube with three small, light, plastic balls in it. I was instructed to blow as hard as I could and see if I could get the three balls to float. If I could get the balls to float long enough, they would take me off the breathing machine and untie me.

That was all I needed to hear. He wouldn't tell me how long I needed to keep blowing, but it didn't matter. I knew I could breathe without this machine and I wanted to prove it. He proceeded to gently remove the breathing tube from my throat while making sure I understood that I would probably need to have it reinserted, and that in a few more hours someone would test me again. I wanted nothing to do with that. I could breathe and I was going to prove it.

At first when he took the breathing tube out, I felt a huge sense of relief. When I tried to talk though, I couldn't do more than mumble. My throat was really sore, but nothing was going to keep me from passing this test. He put the breathing test tube in my mouth; I took the biggest breath I could and blew for all I was worth. Again, I had no idea how long I needed to keep blowing, so I just kept blowing. When there was absolutely no more air in me, I quit.

The nurse shook his head and laughed. In all the years he had been giving this test, no one had come even close to my time. He informed me that I would definitely not need the breathing machine any longer and he proceeded to remove my head from the vice and take the straps off of me. I was free! I had just been through hell and experienced God turn it into heaven. To have experienced all the things I did that night was the greatest gift of my life. A gift from God? No, the gift *was* God!

Chapter 10

Therapy

S hortly after I passed my breathing test, I was
moved to a regular hospital room. I was amazed
at the change I noticed in myself. I appreciated
everything. Every time someone asked me a question and I could answer with a voice that worked, I
felt incredible relief. But the thing I enjoyed most
was that whenever I felt like moving my arm,
I could, and if I wanted to turn my head, I did. I
couldn't believe how much pleasure I took in doing
little things that I'd always taken for granted.

After two days of recovery in my hospital room
on the regular Orthodaedic Floor, Dr. Hackbarth
decided it might be time to transfer me to the
inpatient Physical Medicine and Rehabilitation
service. His colleagues on the Physical Medicine
and Rehabilitation service felt that I would be an
excellent candidate for intense rehabilitation as an

inpatient and accepted my transfer. Little by little we would see if I could walk again, and little by little is exactly how it went. Before I could begin any therapy on my leg, I had to learn how to sit up on my own, get dressed, and get into a wheelchair. It's amazing how hard those things are to do when you can't move your hip.

The therapists gave me an arm extender (a three foot pole with a claw on the end) to grab things that weren't in easy reach. I could really see the wisdom now in God having allowed me to experience being completely immobile. In the past, I would have been discouraged by all this. Here I was, 43 years old and learning how to sit up and dress myself with an arm extender, but because of what I'd been through, I was just happy to be able to move my arms and legs at all.

At first, no matter how hard I tried, I couldn't get dressed on my own, but again I noticed how I had changed. This time when discouragement tried to control my thoughts, it didn't stand a chance. I remember even laughing at the thoughts and thinking *not anymore. You've lost. You're not going to discourage me. Not now. God's bigger than this. Not only am I soon going to be able to sit up and get dressed on my own, before long I'm going to walk again.* The voices of discouragement, depression, and despair kept trying to enter my thoughts, but they just didn't seem very strong anymore and they sure weren't as convincing as they used to be.

I spent about a month in therapy before I was released to go home. While in therapy, I kept thinking about Joan and the boys and how I didn't want to be any more of a burden to them than I had to be. I don't know if they had a more motivated patient then me. My Aunt Irene had recently had her hip replaced and she, along with my cousin Duane, gave me some great advice that I tried to keep in mind. Their advice was simply to do as much as the therapists allowed. No more. Make sure I did whatever they would allow me to do, but no more. There was no point in risking injury.

Whatever the therapists allowed me to do I did. If they said no, I stopped, but I was like a little kid asking for candy in the checkout line. I would ask a number of times before accepting no for an answer. Every once in awhile an exasperated therapist would laugh at me and just say, "No Tim, no." I wanted to walk!

In addition to the walking, there were also a number of flexibility and strength exercises, and I hated almost every one of them. I wanted to be walking, not doing arm and leg lifts. As the days went by, however, I began to understand how important these exercises were for my therapy. Because all of my walking would be with a walker, my arms needed to be strong enough to support me, and all the leg exercises were increasing my leg strength and range of motion. Those exercises were doing just as much (or more) to help me walk and take care of myself as trying to walk was.

I'm definitely the kind of person that needs to know why I'm doing something before I can really put all I have into it, but now that I had my why for these "extra" exercises, I started to put everything I had into them as well. I still hated doing them, and at times it hurt, but I had to trust that my therapists knew what they were doing. As I had done so many times before during this whole cancer experience, I learned to block out the pain and keep going.

Some people have asked me how, when the pain is so intense, do you block the pain out. It's hard to explain, and I know that a big part of it was God's grace on my life, but there were things I purposely did to try to ignore the pain. I'd try to see how many people I could pray for while experiencing the pain. I'd concentrate really hard on the pain and try to decide if it meant something was really hurt and needed medical attention, or if it just came from parts of my body that were tired and sore. If I knew the pain meant I was just tired and sore, it was easier to ignore the pain and keep going.

There were two main things, however, that kept me going no matter how much pain I was in. Number one, I wanted to walk with Joan, Kevin, and Eric again someday, and number two, I wanted to teach again. I was fortunate in that through this whole ordeal, my desire to walk with my family and stand on my own in front of my band again was greater than any degree of pain adversity could throw at me. Probably the way to conquer pain is to want something with a greater intensity than your dislike or fear of the pain.

By the middle of February, I was home again. There were a few setbacks, (At the end of February, I had to go back to Froedtert to have some corrective surgery done on the incision to help it heal properly), but overall everything went as well or better than we could have hoped for. I continued to receive therapy at home, and by the end of April, I had permission from Dr. Hackbarth to begin walking with just the aid of a cane again. That month, I also received clearance from my doctors and the school district to return to teach the following fall. I had made it! Two-and-a-half years after being given a few months to live, I was now more alive than I'd ever been.

There are a number of doors in my life that have been closed due to my battle with cancer, doors that I enjoyed walking through, doors that opened into areas of my life that I'll never again get to experience. But, I have also learned that my life has many doors that I never even knew were there—doors that open into areas of my life that I would have missed out on, areas of my life that I now thoroughly enjoy. Cancer has taken many things from my life, but God has proven his word to be true. He has worked all things in my life together for good; even the cancer.

Chapter 11

New Doors

The old saying "when God closes a door, he opens a window" might very well be true, but I found my experience with cancer to be slightly different. For me, whenever God closed a door, he revealed new doors. All kinds of doors leading to experiences I would have missed out on.

Almost every one of these new experiences included people, along with their support and encouragement. There are many people, such as Rick and Betty Kangas, who I might not have really had the opportunity to know if it wasn't for my cancer and their generous spirit. Betty was a wonderful Sunday School teacher at our church and immediately offered to help when she learned of my cancer.

With Joan teaching piano, the boys had to spend a lot of time by themselves in the evening, and when I wasn't in the hospital, they had to spend a considerable part of their evening taking care of me. Betty and Rick had grown very fond of the boys at church and wanted to help them as much as they could. At least once a week, they would drive to our house after work, make supper, and help the boys with their homework. If there was no homework, out came the games, or Rick would take the boys for rides in his truck.

They didn't do this once or twice. They did this from the beginning of March through the end of May, and when school started again in the fall, Betty and Rick started again with their visits. They would work all day and then come and take care of us until nine or nine-thirty at night. We grew to look forward to their visits so much that the boys and I would find ourselves watching the clock to see how many minutes were left until Rick and Betty would arrive. It just felt good to have them around.

They would listen to how all of us were doing and provide such positive encouragement that we just knew everything would be alright. Before leaving, they would pray. I loved to listen to Rick pray. Always simple and always direct. Straight to the heart of God. Betty would often come with a scripture or a quote that God had laid on her heart for me, and that always went straight to my heart.

Even though Steve and Christy Oswald lived within ten to fifteen minutes of church on the east side of Green Bay, they drove to our house on the west side every Wednesday to make sure Kevin and Eric had the opportunity to attend their church youth groups. They refused all our attempts to give them money and they never missed a Wednesday. One of the fondest memories the boys have from this period of our lives is their time with the Oswalds going back and forth to church.

By April and May of 2002, I had a bad case of cabin fever. I needed to get out of the house, but other than going to the doctor, I couldn't. Between taking care of me, the boys, the house, and teaching, Joan definitely didn't have the time to take me anywhere, and I couldn't drive on my own. I was stuck in the house, except for Tuesdays. Rachel and Kaitlyn Shelter were two young piano students of Joan's, and their mom, Therese, would bring them for lessons each Tuesday. During the lesson, she would take her boys to the park to play. One day, she asked Joan if the boys would like to come along. Of course the answer was yes. She then asked if I wanted to come as well. Of course the answer was again yes.

They all waited patiently for me to get into the front seat of the van and then off we went. Therese and the boys would run off playing in the park and I would sit in the van watching them. It might not seem like much, but at the time it meant the world to me. Every so often, Kevin and Eric would run over to me and tell me to watch something they were going to do, and I watched. I wasn't in my hospital bed away from it all. I was here at the park, with my boys, alive and watching them play. I felt so strong every Tuesday at the park with the Shelters.

One of the first days after Dr. Jaslowski ordered a hospital bed for our living room, one of our Pastors, Rod Zimmerman, came to visit in the morning. Due to the chemo, I was having a really rough morning with nausea, and because of my leg, I was having a tough time getting to the bathroom. He just barely walked in when I knew I was going to throw up again. Without worrying about himself, he helped me out of bed and to the bathroom. I could have thrown up at any time and most likely it would have been on him, but he helped me anyway. After I got back into bed, we visited as if nothing had happened.

He'll probably never understand what that visit meant to me. He didn't have to come, but he did. He didn't have to help me, but he did. He didn't have to treat me as if I was a regular person, but he did. I'll always remember and appreciate him for that.

When Joan and I were in Dr. Jaslowski's office waiting for the results of my first blood test, we realized that we weren't going to make it back to our house before the boys came home from school. Joan remembered that our neighbor, Cathy Caelwaerts, was a nurse in that hospital and thought that Cathy might be finishing her shift soon. We found out what department Cathy worked in and Joan gave her a quick phone call. I'll never forget the concern Cathy showed for all of us as she immediately made plans to bring the boys to her house after school.

Kevin and Eric often played with her two boys after school, so they didn't suspect anything was really wrong. Once Joan and I got home and gave Cathy a call, she offered to watch the boys for the evening while we talked things over and called our families. Cathy would try to catch us at the hospital whenever she could and kept in close contact with us through the whole ordeal. Whenever we needed someone to watch the boys, it would take something really big to keep her from saying yes, and there is not one person anywhere that cheered each of my successes more heartily then Cathy.

In early November of 2003, I was at one of the lowest points in my recovery, living with the belief that I would probably spend the rest of my life in a wheelchair. I could still drive and would often take the boys to school. I took advantage of any excuse to get out of the house. Our mini-van, a 1995 Voyageur with 148,000 miles on it, would need to be replaced soon, but we didn't have the money. We prayed that it would keep running, but it didn't.

On this particular morning, the transmission literally exploded just as we turned a corner. We heard a loud bang and all power to the wheels disappeared. I steered the van to the curb and the boys got out and collected the transmission parts lying all over the road right behind us. I didn't know what to do.

We had the van towed to the repair shop where we have most of our repair work done and got the bad news. Even with used parts, the repair bill would be just under $1400. We definitely didn't have that kind of money. We left the van at the repair shop for a day while we prayed and tried to figure out what to do. We needed the van and realized that we had no choice but to put the repair on the credit card and find a way to pay for it. Joan and I felt very uneasy about going into debt this way, but we couldn't see any other option. We had to leave it in God's hands. Whether we paid the mechanic or the credit card company, the money would have to come from the Lord.

About a week later, Joan and I were again trying to figure out how to pay our credit card bill. Joan went over our entire budget, but there was no extra money. God had already been miraculously providing for us as it was. We each asked the Lord's blessing on our finances and trusted God that we would be able to pay it off as quickly as possible, but we had no idea how quick God would be.

The next day at about four o'clock in the after-noon, our doorbell rang and standing there were two Bay Port band students (seniors Sarah Dushek and Katie Roarty) bearing two incredibly huge smiles and a card. They asked if they could come in and explained what the band had been up to. This was my second Christmas away from the students and they wanted to get me something to make sure I knew they hadn't forgotten me. This alone touched me, but I was totally unprepared for what was to come.

The band students had organized a coin drive to raise money for my Christmas present. There are three bands at Bay Port, and at first the Freshmen band was raising more money than the older students in the Concert Band and Wind Ensemble were. The Wind Ensemble students weren't too happy about this and decided that, no matter what, their band was going to raise the most, but the Freshmen were not about to relinquish their lead. In the middle of all this, the Concert Band, which was the band I conducted, decided that they were my band and that no one was going to out-give them. The music parents wanted to join in and decided that whatever the band students gave, they would match. In the end, the students raised a little over $730, and with the addition of the money from the music parents, Sarah and Katie presented me with a check for around $1,460.

I was stunned when I saw the check. The kids had no idea how desperately we needed that money and we had no idea the students were doing this, but God knew it all. The next time I went to school, I thanked the students as best I could, even though I felt completely inadequate in my ability to show them how much we appreciated what they had done. I didn't want to miss the chance to point out how God had just used them to help someone in need. I remember telling the students in each of the bands that if they ever doubted whether God could use them, to think back to this time and me. God had definitely used each of them for good in my life, and if he did it once, he could do it again.

In March, the music parents decided to take turns bringing meals to us on Sunday afternoons. They sent a sign-up sheet home to see how many families would be interested in joining in. So many families signed up that we had a meal from different families almost every week from the end of March through September. In addition, Joan's piano families would often bring meals with them when they came for lessons or they would just call and say they were coming over with a meal.

At the time I was diagnosed with cancer, Kevin was in third grade and Eric was in kindergarten. Each spring, Kevin had participated in the Forest Glen Elementary School Interest Fair and was looking forward to participating once again. Eric was also excited because this was the first year he would be able to participate. My cancer changed all of that, however. With everything going on in our lives, there was no time for an Interest Fair project. Both boys were, to say the least, very disappointed.

One day, Joan and I were talking with Kevin's teacher, Jenny Emery, about how Kevin was doing in school when we happened to mention how disappointed both he and Eric were with not being able to do a project for the Interest Fair. She offered to help, but we realized it was too late to get a project done even with her, so we dropped the subject.

Jenny, however, did not drop the subject. She started talking with a few other teachers and they arranged for Kevin and Eric to have their own private Interest Fair, complete with participation medals and teacher critiques. As often as possible, Jenny came over to our house and worked with both boys on their projects. Although, work might be too strong a word—it's hard to call anything involving that much laughter work. But work, play, or whatever you want to call it, both boys completed projects and received their participation medals.

I'll never forget how proud the boys were of their projects, and the way they bragged to everyone that they got to work with Miss Emery. It was hard on me, at first, to have someone else working with the boys. That should have been my job, but there was no feeling depressed when Miss Emery was around.

Often as the boys would work on their project, they would come over to my hospital bed (there in the living room) and get my opinion. There were even times, when I felt up to it, that Jenny would help me to the kitchen table where I'd sit and watch them work. Her positive, energetic attitude was contagious and brightened our lives every time she came. I've since learned that that is just who she is. A loving, energetic person that brightens the lives of everyone she comes in contact with.

Yard work has always been a favorite hobby of mine. Knowing that Joan would have to take care of the yard now on top of everything else was really hard on me. The boys were old enough to help, but not to take care of things themselves, so it looked like one more burden would fall on Joan—or so we thought. A number of students offered, or actually insisted on helping with the yard.

I specifically remember Colin and Kaisa McCambridge as they spent two summers making sure our yard was mowed whenever needed. In the spring and fall they would come once a week, and in the heat of the summer they would call every couple of weeks to find out if we needed any work done. I loved the days when Colin and Kaisa came.

As I watched these two kids work in our yard, refusing to take any reimbursement, my world always seemed to brighten. Any life lived with kids like these in it—including mine—couldn't be bad. As we talked, I would try to thank them and tell them how much they meant to me, but they would always turn it around and talk about how I was doing. They offered constant encouragement, applauded every success, and not one visit went by that didn't include the words, "we just want you to get better, Mr. Johnson." How could I let them down? I had to get better! They may never understand how much they meant to my recovery. What they provided was so much more than yard work; they inspired in me an even stronger determination to teach again—to beat this thing and get my life back.

When I went back to teaching in September of 2004, I really wasn't able to pull my share of the load within the band department. We have a very strong band program, and I didn't want to impede the success of the students or add more work to my colleagues' workloads. This didn't seem to be a concern of theirs at all, however.

Each day, my students would ask how I was doing and they made sure no one was a discipline problem for me. As for my fellow band directors, Luther Appel, Sue Zipperer, Tom Kirchen, and Andy Zipperer, they never complained even though I had to take a number of sick days that year, and they made sure that one of them was always in a rehearsal with me in case I started to feel sick and had to step down for a moment. If it wasn't for them, I really doubt that I would have made it through my first year back. I now have a full teaching load again (running the Bay View Middle School band program), but without their concern, compassion, and patience, my dream of returning to teach would never have been realized.

I often thank my students for the respect they have shown me as I've battled my way back. I tell them how happy I would be if there is anything they can learn from my experience. I also remind them that even though they may never have to go through what I have been through, they will all know someone who is, and that hopefully they've been watching Mr. Appel, Mrs. Zipperer, Mr. Kirchen, and Mr. Zipperer. The way each of these teachers treated me is the way they should help those around them who are in need.

As the months have now turned into years since my battle with cancer began, I find it keeps getting easier to understand the love God was actually showing me by allowing the cancer into my life. There are people who mean so much to me now that I wouldn't even know if I hadn't had cancer. In addition, there are things I can now do that I didn't even know were possible for me.

I started playing drums when I was 11 and studied percussion through college and beyond. One of the greatest joys of my life was being able to perform. You'll notice I used the word *was*. That's because I can't really perform as a percussionist anymore. Due to the chemo, the two stem cell transplants, and other various drugs, I have a continual tremor in my right hand that, at times, can become quite noticeable. Other than playing drum rolls, there's not much I can do anymore.

Once again, though, God had a plan. When I got back to work, Tom Kirchen began to help me with my trumpet playing. Tom is a wonderful trumpet player and whenever we had a few minutes, he would answer my questions. Over the course of the next two years, my playing developed to the point where I'm now performing on trumpet and loving it.

My problem was God's opportunity to teach me that:

There is a purpose for problems.
Every problem comes with an opportunity.
God can and will make all things work together for
    good if I'm willing to wait
    while he's making all things work together for
    good.
Problems are nothing to fear.
Depression is real.
Most of my depression is lifted when I come to
    understand how much God loves
    me and how much bigger God is, even if my
    situation does not seem to
    change.
There are always things to be thankful for.
It's hard to be depressed when I'm thankful.
It's useless to try to control God with my words.
It's imperative that God control me with His word.
I can be content, no matter what is happening to me,
    by trusting God.

Chapter 12

Seven-and-a-Half Years Later

It's hard to believe it's been seven-and-a-half years since I was given two or three months to live. Sometimes it's hard to believe all this ever happened at all. Eric is now in seventh grade and has me for a band director at school. Kevin recently turned 16 and has his driver's license. Life is pretty normal. Work is challenging, frustrating, maddening, fantastic, and rewarding. Just like normal. At home there are days in which the whole house seems to be falling apart. There is never enough time and there are always more demands hanging over me then I can come through on. Some things never change.

As I look back over the past seven-and-a-half years, however, I've slowly come to the realization that there has been at least one considerable change—me. I find that now I notice and appreciate little things that before I took for granted. It's not that I wasn't a grateful person before the cancer. I was. I just didn't realize there was so much to be thankful for.

I remember back to a few months after my second stem cell transplant when I went through a vast array of tests to answer questions on how my immune system was doing. Were the new stem cells taking hold and forming a new immune system? Was the new immune system growing stronger and the old immune system weakening? If not, then it was just a matter of time before the cancer would come back and I would suffer a relapse. We all knew the odds of my surviving a second round of cancer were close to zero.

A few days later, Joan and I went back to Milwaukee and nervously waited for the test results. After waiting for a much shorter time then it seemed, one of the Physician Assistants, Paula, came in smiling. She closed the door, turned to me, and said "Everything's going just the way we want it to, Tim. You're probably going to live to see your grandkids." For the next few moments we stood in the middle of the room laughing, crying, and hugging. It's an incredible moment when you realize your body wasn't only taking on Hell, it was defeating it.

Paula went on to mention other moments in life I had to look forward to. Such as being able to work and decide for myself when to retire; being there when Kevin and Eric graduate from high school; getting to meet and know their future spouses. Another milestone she mentioned was being alive to see the boys get their driver's licenses, and on September 15, 2008, I did just that. Kevin passed his driver's test and got his license. This was the first of Paula's "moments" that I could mentally check off, and I savored the moment. I had made it. I had lived to see this. I couldn't get over it. *I'm alive!* I went up to our bedroom, knelt at the side of the bed, and thanked God.

God has restored to me almost everything that was taken away. I can walk. I can play catch with the boys. I can shoot baskets in the driveway. I can mow the yard and weed the garden. When things around the house break, I can fix them. I can climb a ladder to paint the ceiling of the bathroom. I can shop without needing a motorized cart. I can fish from a canoe. (My cousins Dan and Duane even got me in a kayak!) I've been on roller coasters at the Wisconsin Dells, and when the ceiling light in the kitchen needs a new bulb, I can take care of it!

Cancer was God's opportunity to give me what I really needed—a better knowledge of Him and a thankful spirit. There are times now when I just sit quietly and breathe, remembering when I couldn't. Sometimes when I walk from the living room to the bathroom and back, I stop and thank God that this is no longer a twenty-minute journey. When I eat, the food has taste again. I can roll over in bed, yet I know what it's like to be tied down. I can talk when I want, yet I know what it's like to be incapable of communicating. I get dressed and remember when I needed others to dress me. I cook breakfast in the morning and remember when I needed others, or even a machine, to feed me. I have so much to be thankful for.

God has written an incredible story for each one of our lives. My Dad was right; God did know how everything would turn out. He should—after all, He wrote the story. The question never was *could God make the story come true?* The question all along was, *would I be willing to live it?*

I often get up in the middle of the night to pray for Joan and the boys. I love to watch them sleep. I remember the days and nights, the weeks and even months when I wasn't with them, and I thank God that I am here. I enjoyed life before the cancer, but I'm much happier now. I have a long way to go before I can say that "in everything I give thanks," but I know I'm a lot closer to that now than I was before the cancer. Thankful and happy. Those two words might be inseparable.

God doesn't need to explain Himself to us, and it's wrong for us to demand it of Him. But if we let Him, it's through the problems we face that He will reveal Himself. He will reveal His power. He will reveal His love. He will reveal His grace. If we let Him, He will personally say to each of us just as

He did to Moses, "I Am" all you will ever need, no matter what. There is so much to be thankful for!

1. Romans 8:28   And we know that all things work together for good to those who love God, to those who are called according to His purpose.
2. James 5:14   Is anyone among you sick? Let him call for the elders of the church, and let them pray over him, anointing him with oil in the name of the Lord.
3. I Samuel 17
4. Genesis 37
5. Parts of this story can be found in 'The Favor Factor' by Arni Jacobson Charisma House (pg 101-105)
6. John 17:3   And this is eternal life, that they may know You, the only true God, and Jesus Christ whom You have sent.
7. Philippians 4:13

8. Mark 9:23   Jesus said to him, If you can believe, all things are possible to him who believes.
9. Job 1 & 2
10. Acts 5:41
11. Romans 8:37   Yet in all these things we are more than conquerors through Him who loved us.
12. Romans 8:39   ...nor height nor depth, nor any created thing, shall be able to separate us from the love of God which is in Christ Jesus our Lord.

CPSIA information can be obtained at www.ICGtesting.com
Printed in the USA
LVOW061600070312

272040LV00002B/104/P